USER ACCEPTANCE TESTING

BCS, THE CHARTERED INSTITUTE FOR IT

BCS, The Chartered Institute for IT champions the global IT profession and the interests of individuals engaged in that profession for the benefit of all. We promote wider social and economic progress through the advancement of information technology science and practice. We bring together industry, academics, practitioners and government to share knowledge, promote new thinking, inform the design of new curricula, shape public policy and inform the public.

Our vision is to be a world-class organisation for IT. Our 70,000 strong membership includes practitioners, businesses, academics and students in the UK and internationally. We deliver a range of professional development tools for practitioners and employees. A leading IT qualification body, we offer a range of widely recognised qualifications.

Further Information
BCS, The Chartered Institute for IT,
First Floor, Block D,
North Star House, North Star Avenue,
Swindon, SN2 1FA, United Kingdom.
T +44 (0) 1793 417 424
F +44 (0) 1793 417 444
www.bcs.org/contact

USER ACCEPTANCE TESTING
A STEP-BY-STEP GUIDE

Brian Hambling, Pauline van Goethem

Published by BCS Learning and Development Ltd, a wholly owned subsidiary of BCS, The Chartered Institute for IT, First Floor, Block D, North Star House, North Star Avenue, Swindon, SN2 1FA, UK.
www.bcs.org

Paperback ISBN: 978-1-78017-167-8
PDF ISBN: 978-1-78017-168-5
ePUB ISBN: 978-1-78017-169-2
Kindle ISBN: 978-1-78017-170-8

British Cataloguing in Publication Data.
A CIP catalogue record for this book is available at the British Library.

Typeset by Lapiz Digital Services, Chennai, India.
Printed at CPI Antony Rowe Ltd, Chippenham, UK.

CONTENTS

LIST OF FIGURES AND TABLES

AUTHORS

Pauline van Goethem is a freelance UAT and IT training consultant. She has 17 years' experience of change management, testing and training, helping to deliver IT and change management projects in industries as diverse as financial services, energy and utilities and TV and social media. She is a certified tester and Scrum Master and has been employed as a project manager, business analyst, UA tester, UAT manager, end user trainer and UAT trainer. She started her own implementation support company in 2006, specialising in offering training and UAT consultancy and services. Pauline is a member of the International Software Testing Qualification Board (ISTQB) Glossary review team.

Brian Hambling has spent nearly 40 years in the IT industry in a wide variety of development, testing and quality management and project management roles. His first task as a software professional was to acceptance test flight software on behalf of the RAF and he has maintained a strong interest in the achievement of software quality throughout his career. He has been an active member of the testing community through the BCS Special Interest Group in Software Testing, at BCS Professional Certification (formerly ISEB) as Chair of the Software Testing Examination Board, and at the ISTQB as a contributor to examination processes and as an examiner.

INTRODUCTION

This is a book about user acceptance testing (UAT) in its many forms and the uses to which it is put. It draws together many strands of material about testing, project management, quality management, team behaviour and other relevant pieces of the complete UAT experience and weaves them into a strong and reliable lifeline for the novice UA tester or stakeholder.

The book has been written to meet the needs of three disparate groups of people. The first of these groups is those who are directly involved in the UAT exercise. For this group we aim to provide a practical and fairly complete guide to the testing of information systems that contain software. As the subtitle indicates, we have adopted a step-by-step approach to enable them to acquire the necessary terminology (jargon) and basic principles as they learn about the practical challenges of UAT and how to deal with them. Within this group we include not only those asked to do the testing (usually end-users of the system) but also those who will have commissioned the system and the testing (sponsors) and those who will be expected to deliver the expected benefits (business managers). The book addresses this group as a whole, but also identifies the specific challenges and provides a practical guide for each of the subgroups within it.

The second group is the professional testers or developers who have been asked to support UAT, or who may simply wish to better understand why UAT is both important and challenging. For this group we explain what kind of support may be needed and why, and we explain where UAT fits within the overall context of structured testing and development life cycles.

The third group is made up of those professionals for whom UAT is an essential 'tool of the trade'; project managers, quality managers and test managers for example. For this group we seek to place UAT within the overall disciplines of testing, quality management and project management.

Above all the book is intended to explain and explore the significance of an exercise that is commonly neglected in books about testing and often overlooked in books about project management and quality management, yet which is a bridge between these disciplines and, in some respects, is an essential practical expression of each of them.

WHAT THIS BOOK IS ABOUT

Information systems (ISs)

Generally speaking we acquire software to enable us to achieve something of value to us, such as playing a game, making our first million on the stock exchange, or making our business run more efficiently. In some cases software can achieve its purpose without human involvement (except to press a button), but in most cases software interacts with people in a way that achieves a desired result. For example an air traffic control system might provide information to air traffic controllers about where aircraft are, where they are going, how fast and so on. The air traffic controller makes decisions about where each aircraft should go to ensure they are all safely separated and the system relays this information to the pilots of the aircraft. So the purpose of the overall system is to keep aircraft safe and to do that it needs suitably trained people, the air traffic control software, some hardware and some organisation (for example to provide communications between air traffic controllers and pilots). Although this is quite a complex example, it has all the characteristics of an IS. What it most importantly demonstrates is that software is not something that operates in isolation. What users are interested in is not just whether the software does what it should do but whether the system as a whole achieves its purpose and whether they, as users, will be able to operate the system effectively (and without undue stress).

Characteristics of a system

A system is a collection of interdependent components that interact according to a plan to achieve a specific goal.

The key thing to remember about a system is that 'the whole is greater than the sum of the parts'. So a team focused on a goal can achieve much more than the team members could achieve individually if they were not a team.

Interdependence means that every part is vital.

Systems only behave like systems when they have a clear purpose.

Characteristics of an IS

An IS is a system comprising humans, computers, organisation, processes and a single purpose – the business intent.

It is the business intent that makes this collection a system. The components are interdependent, so neither the computers nor the humans can achieve the business intent on their own. Organisation and processes manage the interactions.

When we build or test an IS we must consider all the components, and the interactions, and the common business intent. Figure 0.1 provides a schematic view of an IS for a business.

Figure 0.1 An information system

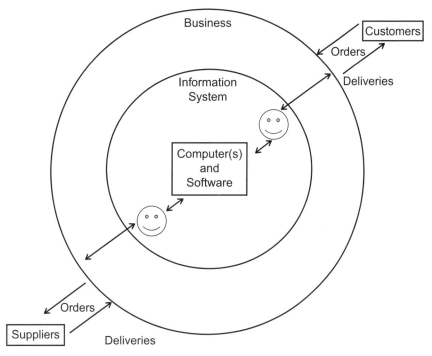

In a business context we would have business processes that involve human beings using information to add business value, such as a supermarket checkout assistant adding up all the retail values of the items purchased by a customer, preparing a bill for the customer to pay, accepting payment and providing a receipt. All of this could be done manually, but this is a process that is usually automated for reasons of efficiency and for the advantage of having all the details of each transaction available as information to be processed in making other decisions such as when to restock. In this example the effectiveness of the overall process would probably be measured by how quickly and accurately a single customer's shopping can be handled. Here again the whole process is measured, not just the part the software does, because that is the process that adds value to the business. From a user perspective a checkout operator will be sitting at a checkout for perhaps hours at a stretch. To them it will be vitally important that the efficient operation of the checkout is achievable routinely and without heroic effort. If the scanner refused to scan some items, the conveyor broke down at regular intervals or the bills produced were even occasionally incorrect, the impact on the user would undoubtedly be increased stress.

So this book is about testing ISs and not just software, and it is also about considering all the perspectives of all the people involved in building, operating and using the system to achieve its expected business benefits.

Testing ISs

When we set up a UAT exercise we are testing a system and not just a piece of software, which means we are really interested in knowing whether the overall IS works. If the system does not work as we expect, there could be a number of reasons, and among these is the possibility that the software does not do what it should. But the software could be working perfectly and some other aspect of the system could be at fault.

To make this as clear as possible we need to take a brief look at how ISs are created – not in detail but as a high-level view of what happens to an IS from the first idea through to the realisation. This high-level perspective is usually called a life cycle.

The life cycle of an IS is simply a model of everything that happens to it from the time it is first envisaged to the time it is retired. Figure 0.2 shows a simple schematic view of what an IS life cycle might look like.

What this life-cycle model describes is a process that begins with requirements (which are the means of describing what the system needs to do), proceeds through a vague and shadowy phase called development (which we will only delve into occasionally and only if we absolutely need to understand something about it) before reaching UAT as the final stage before the system is 'released' into service. We will take a closer look at how requirements are arrived at and documented in Chapter 2.

Figure 0.2 Life cycle of an IS

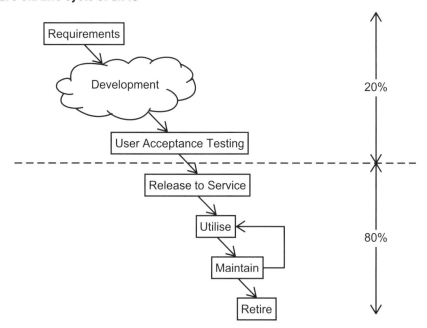

One key feature of this life cycle is the balance of time, effort and money spent on it. The part of the life cycle that usually gets most of the attention is the initial development, even though that accounts for only about 20 per cent of the total spend. Most of a system's life is spent in being used, maintained, modified and repaired. The better the system is at the end of development, the lower that large chunk of life-cycle cost is likely to be – and the 'gatekeeper' between development and the rest of the life cycle is UAT. Effective UAT can avoid excessive maintenance costs (for example repairing defects), reduce the cost of modifications (for example to improve the system's usability) and prolong the life of the system, so giving a better return on the original investment in development.

UAT is the final frontier between initial development and the rest of the system's life, a frontier beyond which could be a world in which your new IT system makes your life easier, anticipates your needs, saves you time and always turns out great results – or a world where using your IT system is a nightmare in which nothing functions, the system seems determined to prevent you completing your work and the outputs are never what you wanted.

Anyone accustomed to using IT systems knows that these two 'parallel universes' are actually very close together and that predicting which of those worlds you will be transported to when your system is declared operational is not easy. That is the role of UAT – to provide a glimpse of the future (just) in time to avert a disaster if that is what you foresee and to give the users the best possible start with using the system.

THE ROLE OF UAT

UAT is a test of an IS from the perspective of the users and other stakeholders for whom it has been built or acquired. UAT is not just a test of the software, nor of the functionality, performance, reliability and security, nor of the usability of the system. That does not mean UAT is not concerned with any or all of those areas, but that its primary concern and absolute focus is on whether or not the system can deliver the expected business benefits when operated by its designated users. All of the specialist areas mentioned will have, or certainly should have, been tested during development. None of those tests, however, answers the question 'Is the system fit for purpose?' UAT answers that question unequivocally by testing it against the reason it was built or acquired, using the eventual end-users as testers and, as far as possible, utilising the user documentation prepared to support their use of the system. This will entail not just exercising the system in some random or even structured way; it will entail using the system to enable business processes that deliver value using realistic (or actual) scenarios, data and operations. UAT is the nearest we get to 'the real thing' without actually taking the risk of releasing the system into service, and it is the exercise that will enable us to make a rational judgement about whether to take the risk of releasing it into service.

THE COSTS AND BENEFITS OF UAT

UAT is an expensive exercise. As well as the hard costs of actually doing the testing, we have to factor in the additional time that development resources are tied up before roll-out of the system allows them to be released to other projects.

The largest components of the direct cost of UAT are:

- The cost of diverting end-user staff from their normal work to plan and carry out UAT. As well as salary costs there is the loss of whatever revenue the staff would have generated or the delay in realising that revenue.
- The cost of training or familiarisation for the UAT team (and subsequently for all end-users).
- The cost of test environments for UAT.

A UAT exercise with a team of six staff that takes two weeks to complete might have direct costs of around £6,000–£10,000 for salaries alone.

What do we have to offset this cost?

THE VALUE OF UAT – THE REASONS WE NEED TO DO IT

In case you are not convinced of the need to go to the time and expense of a UAT exercise, we will take a brief look at the world of ISs and what can go wrong with them.

Reason 1: risk management – avoiding expensive failures

HIGH-PROFILE IT FAILURES

US trading systems, unable to cope with the number of transactions, fail causing panic among sellers.
On Friday 17 October 1987, after a number of Securities and Exchange Commission (SEC) investigations of insider trading and the London stock market closing due to severe weather conditions, it looked like a sustained period of growth was going to come to a sudden halt for the US stock market. On Black Monday the crash started in Far Eastern markets and, after a weekend of worrying about their shares, investors sold stock in a mass exodus of the market, generating a flood of sell orders and crashing trading systems. As a result more than 20 per cent was wiped off the value of the US stock market in a single day.

A new computer system means 500,000 UK passports cannot be issued on time.
In the summer of 1999 the UK Passport Agency brought in a new Siemens computer system without sufficiently testing it or sufficiently training staff on how to use it. At the same time an unusually high demand for passports was driven by a change in the law, which meant that children under the age of 16 required their own passport when travelling abroad. As a result the Home Office had to pay millions in compensation for missed holidays and staff overtime.

A memory leak in the London Ambulance Service's new emergency dispatch system leaves 46 people dead.
Before 1992, office staff decided what ambulances should be dispatched where and it seemed that there were efficiencies that could be achieved by using a

computerised system. Just a few hours after it was deployed problems began to arise with the new system. The root cause of the main breakdown of the system was a memory leak in a small portion of code. The system retained memory about incident information on the file server even after it was no longer needed. As with any memory leak, after enough time, the memory filled up and caused the system to fail. The next day, the Ambulance Service switched back to a part-manual system, and shut down the computer system completely when it stopped working altogether eight days later. In those nine days the lives of up to 46 people might have been saved had an ambulance been able to get to them in time.

Microsoft rushes to release a flawed games console to stay ahead of the competition. The Xbox 360 games console was released by Microsoft in November of 2005, just ahead of Nintendo's PlayStation. It quickly became clear that the Xbox was subject to a number of technical problems and failures; a series of glowing red lights flashing on the face of the console, later nicknamed the 'Red Ring of Death', being the most well known. It was not until 5 July 2007 that Microsoft published an open letter recognising the console's problems, as well as announcing a three-year warranty for every Xbox 360 console that experienced the general hardware failure. The design issues were alleged to be the end results of management decisions and inadequate testing resources prior to the console's release.

Not all ISs end in high-profile failure; many are highly successful and trouble free over a long life, but it is nevertheless true that the statistical likelihood of failure for an IS is relatively high.

In 1995 The Standish Group published a report based on research into a large number of failures in software systems. It was called the CHAOS report (The Standish Group has never revealed what the acronym stands for, only conceding that a few select people in the organisation know) and it contained some frightening statistics, for example that only 16.2 per cent of IS projects were completed on time and on budget. Worse still, completion often required significant watering down of the original specification for these systems.

The statistics relate to system failures and these are not necessarily related to UAT, but the CHAOS report analysed their statistical evidence and identified key factors that contributed to failure. These factors point to problems in some aspects of system development that UAT can throw some light on, such as lack of user involvement and poorly defined requirements.

The original CHAOS report was published quite a long time ago, but The Standish Group has repeated its research and published updated results over a number of years. The results have gradually been improving with the introduction of agile project models and a greater awareness of the issues that cause projects to fail. The 2011 edition of the CHAOS report found that 37 per cent of all projects succeeded and Jim Johnson, Chairman of The Standish Group, stated, 'This year's results represent the highest success rate in the history of the CHAOS research. We clearly are entering a new understanding of why projects succeed or fail.' Although the results show a significant improvement on the original 1995 figures, it is a sobering thought that, even with these unprecedented results, 63 per cent of projects in the study did not succeed. Although other researchers have criticised The Standish Group for providing little or no context to its figures, for instance by not distinguishing between projects where going over the deadline means failure and those where an reasonable overrun can be easily tolerated, nevertheless the CHAOS report presents a very useful list of the key factors that contribute to project failures, the knowledge and application of which can benefit any project. We shall explore some of these factors and how we can learn from them in Chapter 1.

Avoiding high-profile disasters or even low-profile mishaps is not solely about performing effective UAT of course. By the time we get to UAT the seeds of failure have not only been sown, they may well have already germinated; but well-planned UAT may still be able to highlight the potential for disaster before it actually happens. This is an important reason, but not the only one, for doing UAT.

Reason 2: confidence building – achieving expected business benefits

If we have acquired some expensive software or some software designed to do something really important for our business, we need to be sure before we accept it that we have minimised the risk of it not doing the job we acquired it for. This is not just a repetition of disaster avoidance, but a form of 'good housekeeping' that ensures we have addressed all the things that could go wrong when we start to use the system. Many of these may be only small things, but they can add up to a problem in service, and some of these smaller issues may not have been addressed by the testing done during development, which was designed to ensure the system meets its specification rather than ensuring that the users will be able to use it effectively. In Chapter 3 we will show how risk-based testing can be used to minimise the risk.

We will also need to be sure that the people who use the software will get the expected productivity or other benefits and that the business will get the efficiency or other improvements we intended. To do this we need to put the system to use in a realistic environment and work through some examples of situations in which it is expected to add value, such as streamlining processes or reducing the cost of production. This kind of testing will be based on an understanding of how the system will be used to gain business benefits and setting up a realistic 'trial' to see that it is capable of delivering those benefits. We explain in Chapter 6 how we can set up this kind of test.

Reason 3: assessment – getting the business processes right

As well as making sure that the system will not only do what it is supposed to do but will also be usable by our staff, we need to give the end-users an opportunity to exercise the system in whatever way they have agreed to work to make it effective. Users will need to check system behaviour as part of the overall business processes, using it in the way that has been agreed. We will not only treat the system as an IS and test its behaviour when the intended business transactions are passed through it, but we will also test that end-users can operate the system in the way that is needed to make those processes work effectively.

One further benefit of UAT is that the act of determining a system's fitness for purpose necessarily involves comparing the system's behaviour with user expectations. If the comparison is done systematically and formally, then the primary 'result' of UAT may be to accept or not to accept the system. A valuable secondary result, though, is that the comparison will have generated a detailed understanding of how well the system matches expectations. This comparison can be made the basis of an assessment of the system's current capability and value to the business, which in turn can be used to underpin a strategy for future development or enhancement. It enables us to know exactly what the strengths and weaknesses of the system are and to assess value for money and potential for improving business value from the investment in development.

Reason 4: preparation – assessing readiness for service

Finally we want to be sure that the software is fit to release into the business and that the business is ready to make use of it, so we will need to assess readiness. After we have completed the testing based on risks, benefits and usability, we may have discovered some problems that need to be resolved, some defects that need to be corrected or some other aspect that needs to be addressed (such as training). The combination of these things will have an impact on when a system will be completely ready for the users to take on. This aspect of readiness is about how robust the system is in operation, how closely it fits expectations, how many 'workarounds' have been found necessary and a host of other factors that may affect whether or not the system is ready to deliver value to the business. This is usually a matter of discussion and negotiation, and results in a decision to release the software. Chapter 9 will explore the mechanisms we can put in place to make that decision as objective as possible. If we consider this aspect of UAT well in advance (as we should), we can define a set of acceptance criteria that will be used to come to a decision about release and so avoid the conflicts that can arise at this stage.

One important thing to say in this context is that UAT is distinct from training, familiarisation and all other aspects of roll-out. It has its own set of objectives that would be seriously jeopardised if UAT was carried out by unprepared, untrained end-users who were unfamiliar with the system. Having said that, however, the experience of UAT will be a learning exercise that is second to none and the experience gained during UAT can be captured and utilised in training, familiarising and preparing the end-user population for using the system effectively – including dealing with any issues raised by UAT for which 'workarounds' have been defined.

THE ENIGMA OF SOFTWARE

It is always difficult to pin down the cost of software, but it is true that the case usually made for acquiring software – that it saves staff costs – has been shown to be invalid in most cases. Software is expensive to acquire and operate over its complete life cycle from inception to disposal.

A second key characteristic of software is its inflexibility. We imagine software to be very elastic, so that we can change it at will, but this is far from the truth. While it is very easy to change a line of code (in the sense that code can be updated at almost no cost because it is electronic and lives on a machine that can alter its contents instantly), it is very difficult to change the behaviour of a software application in a way that has no negative consequences and meets all our expectations. Software is actually very inflexible as a tool for achieving a business purpose. Once installed the cost and impact of modification can be, and often is, very high.

Thirdly, software is not visible. It has no moving parts and so has nothing that we can see operating. When it stops working it does not 'break' in the way that physical systems do. The computers usually keep operating and doing something; they just stop doing what we want them to. This can be very frustrating especially if we find that the software is not malfunctioning at all, but just responding to some unexpected input.

These three characteristics make software a difficult medium to work with and a difficult business tool to operate unless it is working exactly as we expect it to.

The enigmatic nature of software as a medium makes the risk associated with deploying ISs containing software significant and UAT is the best mechanism we have for managing that risk for the user community. We have already stated that the main reason why UAT is a worthwhile exercise is that it can help to avoid some of the costs of dealing with failures and of modifying the software after its acceptance. The potential costs of failure can be judged from the case study examples, but the cost of failure is invariably higher than expected in a business context because of the ramifications of failure in the tightly knit relationship between business processes and ISs.

There is also one other major benefit from UAT. The skills and newly acquired experience, combined with the invaluable experience that stakeholders bring with them to UAT, have enormous potential value in preparing for and achieving a painless roll-out. Beyond that, the insights gained by those spending time in testing a system can be harnessed to enhance future business process development, training and support. There is potentially a massive benefit to be reaped from the experience of UAT for the individuals concerned and for the business as a whole.

STAKEHOLDERS – WHO THIS BOOK IS FOR

This book is aimed at the groups of people who together comprise the principal stakeholders of UAT:

- sponsors (typically owners or senior managers who have decided to acquire software of some kind to enhance their business);
- business managers, who will be responsible for ensuring the IS delivers the expected business benefits;
- end-users, who will be most interested in the way they are able to interact with the system to achieve their tasks;
- professional developers and testers, who will be concerned with providing the most effective support for UAT;
- managers of processes, practices and standards, who will take an interest in making UAT a cost-effective process using best practice.

In each of these groups there may be some who have no experience of testing at all and for whom an assignment to a UAT team is a daunting prospect.

If you are in this category then this book is for you, and it speaks to you very directly:

- by using non-technical language wherever possible;
- by assuming no prior knowledge of testing at all;
- by identifying what you need to do in a step-by-step fashion;
- by providing case studies, examples and exercises for you to practise at least some of the tasks.

If you are a sponsor and are in the process of acquiring a new IS, the book will identify the role of UAT in ensuring you get the system you are expecting, but it will also help you to understand how UAT fits into your overall planning and what benefits it brings in terms of training and supporting the inevitable change to working practices that new ISs invariably bring.

If you are a business manager who will be responsible for the effective operation of the system in achieving business benefits, the book will explain how those benefits are defined and measured and how you can ensure UAT is shaped to provide you with the information you need to prepare for the system's release into service in your part of the business.

If you are an end-user tasked with testing an IS, the book will provide you with all the tools and techniques you will need to be an effective UA tester.

If you are in the group of 'interested professionals' who may need to support UAT, you will find in this book a clear exposition of how and where the world of UAT interfaces with the work of professional developers and testers and how best to manage that interface and support the UAT activity.

Finally, if your role involves managing and enhancing practice of some kind as a test manager, quality manager or project manager, you will find the book useful as a manual of key techniques, methods and tools. Quality managers wanting to improve UAT practices, for example, will find here a comprehensive review of UAT from which best practice can be distilled and then customised to fit your organisational culture, size and budget.

HOW TO GET THE BEST FROM THIS BOOK

The two main premises of this book are:

1. We can and must make UAT effective to reduce the risk and cost of underperforming ISs.
2. The benefits of UAT outweigh the costs.

To explain why and how these results can be achieved the book has been structured as described below.

The first three chapters provide all the background and justification for a step-by-step approach to UAT:

- Chapter 1 – The Importance of UAT;
- Chapter 2 – Business Requirements;
- Chapter 3 – Testing Basics for UAT.

The next two chapters are dedicated to the practical issues of creating, shaping, training and deploying an effective UAT team:

- Chapter 4 – The UAT Team;
- Chapter 5 – UAT as Transition.

The remaining chapters explain the step-by-step approach in practical detail:

- Chapter 6 – Preparing for UAT – Planning;
- Chapter 7 – Test Design for UAT;
- Chapter 8 – Implementing the Tests;
- Chapter 9 – Evaluating the System;
- Chapter 10 – Life after UAT.

We sincerely hope that all readers of the book will find it interesting and rewarding enough to want to read it from cover to cover. However, the first encounter with any book of this kind needs some kind of plan to extract the maximum value in the minimum time to provide a starting point from which a more detailed exploration of the content can begin. The initial route through the book naturally depends on your starting point.

All readers are strongly advised to read Chapters 1–3 as general background and as preparation for the practical approach later in the book.

Those responsible for managing a UAT team should read Chapters 4 and 5, and all those selected to take part in UAT will gain an understanding of the skills needed and the style of operation for a UAT team by reading these two chapters.

All readers are encouraged to read Chapters 6–10 although some chapters will be more relevant to some groups than to others. Within these chapters all of the stakeholders are considered and information of particular importance to one group or another is labelled appropriately to guide your initial reading.

CHECKLISTS

Whatever approach you take to reading the book you will be guided through all the key steps in UAT through Chapters 6 – 10. Your reading should help you to understand what the key steps are and why they are ordered as they are.

To help you in applying what you learn from the book, you will find a set of checklists for all the major steps in UAT at Appendix A. The purpose of the checklists is to present the key steps in a logical order, uncluttered by explanation, but also indicate where you can find supporting material in the book. We hope you will find these useful when you come to apply the step-by-step approach to your projects.

CASE STUDIES

Throughout the book we will make use of case studies, examples and exercises. The case studies are used to provide documented real-life examples of the things we are talking about; the examples will give you practical guidance on how to use the techniques, methods and approaches we present; the exercises will provide you with opportunities to try out some of the techniques.

In addition to these in-text components we end each chapter with a few multiple-choice questions that you can use as a check that you have understood the key ideas in the chapter and we also provide you with questions that you might like to think about. These raise some of the issues and challenges that you might face as a user acceptance (UA) tester and give you an opportunity to think about them before you have to deal with any real challenges in a project context. We have provided answers to all the exercises in Appendix B so you can check your answers against ours. The more open-ended questions at the end of the chapters have no correct answer, but we have included some of our own thoughts on these questions that you can read if you want to. We make no claims about these being the best responses to the questions, but they are the ones that we have developed from our experience.

Finally, before we progress on to Chapter 1 and take the first step in introducing the UAT process, we are going to introduce you to a small imaginary company called HMF that is acquiring an IS. We will use the HMF case study mainly to wrap around the more significant examples we provide, especially in Chapters 6–9, to provide continuity of ideas and hopefully to help you see how information is built up at each step of the approach for use in later stages.

CASE STUDY – HMF AND THE EXCELSIOR SYSTEM

HMF is a web-based insurance company offering low-cost insurance solutions for a broad range of domestic and commercial risks. HMF has rapidly developed its product range by acquiring smaller specialised insurance providers and integrating their specialised products into its own platform.

HMF has recently conducted a rationalisation programme to ensure that staff numbers and skills are optimal for the integrated product range and to harmonise processes across the business. The rationalisation exercise revealed that accounting and human resource (HR) practices had become fragmented after multiple acquisitions and integrations, and a decision was taken to develop an IS to support common accounting practices across the business and, as a secondary objective, to enhance HR process integration. At the heart of the IS a new software package, known as Excelsior, was specified to run on existing HMF servers.

The Excelsior accounting system was commissioned as a custom-built accounting solution based on a collection of standard accounting modules configured in an architecture that supports full integration of all the modules' services and also enables selected HR applications to be incorporated. The development will be incremental to allow basic functions to become well established before adding further complexity and the first incremental delivery is now ready for UAT. At the current stage of development the accounting functions available will be:

- general accounting;
- purchase orders;
- contracts;
- payments.

In addition the following HR services will be available:

- absence (to book days off, sickness and other absence and manage requests for absence for a team);
- expenses (to enable submission of expenses forms and receipts for payment and to approve expenses related to a team);
- changing contact and bank details and updating personal details held by HR;
- internal purchase orders (request purchases and approve purchases related to a team, marking a purchase order as fulfilled);
- training (request training, take online training, record training attendance);
- administration (support and managerial functionality);
- jobs (search for, list or apply for vacancies, approve applications related to a team).

Each module has a unique title related to Excelsior, for example Excelsior – Training.

Every service is listed on the main menu on the Excelsior home page but access is restricted for some modules. Users are granted access to services based on their role-based login profile. Where access is denied, a link appears that allows users to request access from the appropriate person.

We hope you find HMF and Excelsior, and all the case studies, examples, exercises and the questions at the chapter ends, helpful in bringing the ideas to life and enabling you to gain some insight into what is happening during a real UAT exercise.

1 THE IMPORTANCE OF UAT

The introduction presented some general concepts that help to get a better understanding of UAT and introduced examples of high-profile project failures that, if not caused by UAT, were certainly not prevented by it. Chapter 1 provides an overview of UAT, its purpose and its relationship to an implementation project and the people who take part in it. You will find out why UAT is different from other types of testing and yet often uses the same processes – one of which is the fundamental test process. Finally you will discover what the different types of UAT are, who the stakeholders of UAT are and what each role has to offer to and to gain from the UAT process.

Topics covered in this chapter

- What is UAT?
- Why test information systems?
- Business vulnerability
- The UAT process
- From UAT to service delivery
- UAT and contracts
- Stakeholders in UAT

WHAT IS UAT?

UAT stands for user acceptance testing and is commonly used to refer to the end-user software testing carried out prior to a new information system (IS) being introduced to an organisation. The primary objective of UAT is to ensure the new system does what it set out to do and meets the requirements the business has of it. Here is a definition of the term UAT taken from the ISTQB Glossary of Testing Terms:

Formal testing with respect to user needs, requirements, and business processes, conducted to determine whether or not a system satisfies the acceptance criteria and to enable the user, customers or other authorized entity to determine whether or not to accept the system.

THE INTERNATIONAL SOFTWARE TESTING QUALIFICATIONS BOARD (ISTQB)

ISTQB provides certification at Foundation, Advanced and Expert levels for software testers. The certificates are supported by a glossary available free from www.istqb. org/downloads/glossary.html. We will use the ISTQB Glossary throughout this book because it is widely used in the testing community and in tester certification programmes.

You may also find the following related books, which also use the ISTQB Glossary, helpful if you want to increase your knowledge of testing: *Software Testing: an ISTQB-ISEB Foundation Guide* by Brian Hambling (Ed), Peter Morgan, Angelina Samaroo, Geoff Thompson and Peter Williams; *Software Testing: An ISEB Intermediate Certificate* by Brian Hambling and Angelina Samaroo.

Three aspects of this definition are important and will drive what we do in preparing and implementing UAT:

1. UAT requires 'formal testing', which means that tests should be designed and executed in a structured way that provides objective evidence of the acceptability or otherwise of the system.
2. The definition speaks of testing with respect to 'user needs, requirements, and business processes'. It does not mention any particular specification document but it does draw attention to what users need and it goes beyond testing software to include business processes.
3. The definition speaks of satisfying 'acceptance criteria', which define what is acceptable to the users.

We will explore all three of these key ideas in the book and we will be developing our UAT around acceptance criteria and formal testing of user needs and business processes.

Although other testing takes place before UAT is carried out, UAT is unique in that it is the first time the completed system is tested by users against user needs. Testing during development is based on ensuring that what is delivered matches the corresponding technical specification, but the fit between an IS and its business users is more intimate and it is the unique user perspective that can identify the problems of fitness for purpose in a business context. Without it a system that has been tested by developers and professional testers, and which has passed every test, can still fail at the first hurdle of real use.

That is why UAT needs to include 'end-to-end' testing that exercises complete business processes, including the computer system, rather than testing the computer system in isolation (Figure 1.1). For example in an online retail system, a test of the ordering process must check that an order placed by a customer is accepted and that it triggers identifying, packaging and shipping of the correct product. But these processes must trigger other processes to complete a transaction, for example that the order generates and sends a correct invoice and that payment received is correctly matched with the invoice to close the transaction. Although the scenario is simple, this is a fairly complex set of interacting processes and there is also a time lapse between the initial order and the payment of the invoice, so a full end-to-end test of the transaction will need to follow an order through the system and over time to ensure all the necessary interactions happen correctly and produce a successful result.

Figure 1.1 End-to-end testing of a transaction in an online retail system

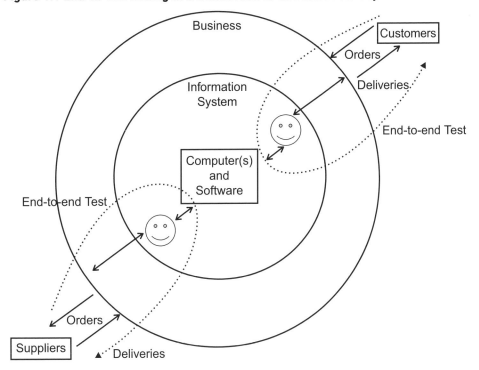

WHY TEST ISs?

Software is one of the greatest examples of human creativity and endeavour. The growth in what can be achieved with computers and software in recent decades has been phenomenal and the trend is likely to continue. Software and software-based systems such as IS are becoming ever more endemic in business life. As the complexity and subtlety of the relationship between IS and business increase, so the impact of failure, by which we mean any mismatch between what an IS actually does and what we need it to do, becomes greater.

This increase in the risk of using an IS must be balanced by increased attention to risk management. There are many facets of risk management but, in the world of software and IS, testing remains one of the key risk management disciplines. As software has become more complex, testing has had to become more effective at identifying problems and potential problems so that they can be resolved before a system fails. As we will explain in Chapter 3, where the sophistication of development activity has increased, testing has also had to become more sophisticated. Why? Because with greater complexity comes greater risk of human mistakes in design and in implementation; because greater integration between human activity and the systems that enable it brings more opportunities for mismatch; and because the many essential characteristics of ISs (such as reliability, usability and security) all need to be assured before the system can be trusted to deliver its services in a real business situation.

The increased dependence of business on IS has also made the relationship between systems and business processes more critical to business success, and in many cases the desired behaviour of an IS cannot be adequately described in technical specifications. Most testing during development is based on ensuring that what is delivered matches the corresponding technical specification, but the fit between an IS and its business users is more intimate and more critical than the fit between craftspeople and their tools; it is rather more like the fit of a garment that is 'made to measure' so that an individual can work comfortably and effectively in it all day and every day. Whether that kind of fit has been achieved is not something that can be determined by anyone other than the user. That is why UAT is different from all other kinds of testing and also why users must take part in it. It is the unique user perspective that can identify the problems of fitness for purpose in a business context and, without it, a system that has been tested by developers and professional testers, and which has passed every test, can still fail at the first hurdle of real use.

REASONS WHY WE NEED TO TEST

The fact that we live in an imperfect world is, at the most basic level, why we may have trouble creating a perfect IS and why it is important to test them.

There may be many reasons why requirements do not exist at all or are not complete and up to date:

- It is often hard for the sponsor or end-users to imagine what their requirements are going to be. Ideas about what the system should become change over time and in the context of development.

- Even when the requirements are clear in the minds of the sponsor or end-user, they may have trouble communicating the requirement. What is written in the requirements document may therefore not reflect what was intended.

- If the requirements reflect what was intended by the sponsor or end-user, the developers may interpret requirements incorrectly because they will bring their own assumptions to the process.

- Even if correctly imagined, communicated, written and interpreted, developers may make mistakes when writing the code that creates the functionality described in the requirements because they are human and therefore fallible.

All of these have been cited as significant issues in studies of why systems fail.

BUSINESS VULNERABILITY

The relationship we have with IS in business is a unique one. In most cases the system does not just make our lives a little easier; it actually carries on some or all of our business processes in a way that may be difficult or even impossible to do manually once the system is in place. The intimate relationship between businesses and the ISs that serve them makes us particularly vulnerable when a system is first introduced or when it is changed or updated. The term 'business critical' is often used for systems that have a significant impact on the way a business operates and delivers its services. To be clear, this is not just about avoiding high-profile failure; it is about ensuring that each and every time we initiate a new IS or change the relationship between a business and its IS, we take care that the new relationship will be as we expected and planned it to be.

The UAT process is the last, and arguably the most important check, before an IS is rolled out. ISs are becoming more and more embedded in business processes and in delivery of business value and, as a result, they are also becoming more complex. The combination of the complexity and business criticality of ISs leaves little margin for error.

THE CHAOS REPORT – THE STANDISH GROUP

The Standish Group was formed in1985 by a group of IT professionals whose aim was to collect case information on real-life IT failures in order to improve IT project success rates. The original CHAOS report, published in 1994, examined 8,380 projects in order to determine whether they were successful and, if not, what the causes of the failures were. The report found the following percentages of projects were successful, unsuccessful or impaired:

- Successful projects completed on time, within budget, containing all the features and functions initially specified – 16 per cent.
- Challenged projects completed and working, but over budget, over time and offering fewer features and functions than initially specified – 53 per cent.
- Impaired projects cancelled at any point during the development cycle or not used post-completion – 31 per cent.

The report also identified the reasons for the failures, listed from the most often occurring to the least often occurring:

1. incomplete requirements;
2. lack of user involvement;
3. lack of resources;
4. unrealistic expectations;
5. other;
6. lack of executive support;

7. changing requirements and specifications;
8. lack of planning;
9. did not need it any longer;
10. lack of IT management;
11. technology illiteracy.

The 2011 edition of the CHAOS Manifesto, an annual report from The Standish Group that examines trends in software project success, found that in a marked improvement on the 1994 figures 37 per cent of all projects succeeded, 42 per cent of projects were challenged and the remaining 21 per cent were considered a failure. Notably, however, the majority of projects are still challenged or impaired according to their findings.

Not all the reasons listed are relevant to UAT, but those that are relevant will be at the forefront of our thinking when planning and executing UAT activities.

The massive disruption to NatWest Group customers following a routine update to its software is an example of what can happen when systems do not perform as expected in a business-critical environment such as banking. The introduction of a new baggage-handling system for Heathrow Airport's new Terminal 5 is another recent example.

THE HEATHROW TERMINAL 5 OPENING

In March 2008 Willie Walsh, CEO of British Airways (BA), gave evidence to the House of Commons Transport Committee about the problems with the opening of London Heathrow Airport's Terminal 5. In his evidence he said:

> ... we had compromised on the testing regime as a result of delays in completing the building programme and the fact that we compromised on the testing of the building did impact on the operation of T5 in the first few days after its opening.

In the first five days of operation the cost to BA of the operational problems was estimated at £16 million and a total of 23,205 bags were 'misconnected'. The extensive delays experienced by passengers, the sight of the unfinished buildings and the problems caused by delays and unprepared staff also caused embarrassment to BA, the British Airports Authority (BAA) and the UK government (House of Commons Transport Committee 2008). One of our main aims in this book is to explain why these kinds of outcomes happen and how they can be avoided.

Meticulous planning, use of highly experienced and competent practitioners and good project management are all essential to success, but they are not enough. We need to know exactly what will happen from the point when the first real user logs on to a system, and no amount of time and money spent on modelling, problem solving, focus groups, contingency planning or any other discipline will tell us what we need to know as effectively as a well-planned, well-structured and well-designed UAT. The immediate cost of failure (£16 million in a few days in BA's case) and the ongoing impact on a business of even a small interruption in a key service, such as paying bills through a bank, have a huge impact – significant enough to cause even large companies to fail.

It is important to understand at this stage that although UAT has so far been described as the activity that can verify the usefulness of the new IS and save a project from going horribly wrong, UAT may not be perceived as such by others. UAT is sometimes perceived as an expensive evil that interrupts 'business as usual', diverts important staff, and costs a disproportionate amount of time and money. The number of high-profile failures associated with releasing software systems that were not ready ensures that most organisations make at least some attempt at an acceptance test, often by pressing reluctant users into an activity in which they feel well outside their 'comfort zone'. Does this have to be the case? Can we make UAT an exercise that is independent of the IT community that built the system yet in partnership with it to achieve the best possible result? The premise of the book as a whole is that we can.

Before we embark on UAT we need to be sure that the cost and effort are worthwhile and we also need to understand the activity well enough to do the best job with the fewest resources. If we understand the activities of UAT well enough to carry them out effectively, the parties involved in UAT should be well prepared, the testing should prove the usefulness of the system and little testing time should be wasted or subject to delay.

THE UAT PROCESS

The process we will describe in this book will take you through each stage of achieving successful UAT in a step-by-step fashion. We will first explain enough background to enable you to see how the parts of the process fit together and we will provide you with tools and techniques that you will need to do your testing. Next we will describe how to recruit and prepare an effective UAT team. Finally we will take you through the stages of a UAT project, again step by step, so that you can apply all the tools and techniques at the right time and in the right way. The basic process is shown in Figure 1.2 and it is based around the fundamental test process as defined in the ISTQB Glossary so that you can compare it with other testing processes you may read about elsewhere.

Figure 1.2 The process of UAT

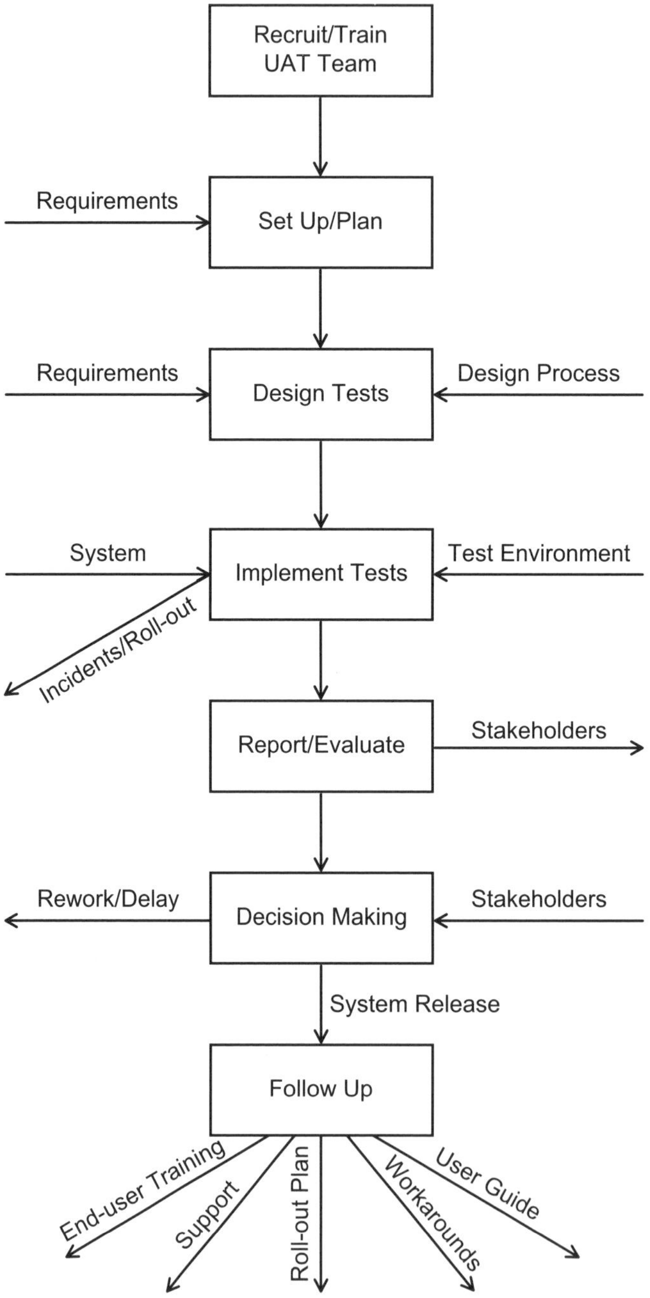

The fundamental test process (FTP) has five stages.

The fundamental test process (FTP)

The ISTQB Glossary describes the FTP as comprising five test stages:

1. test planning and control;
2. test analysis and design;
3. test implementation and execution;
4. evaluating exit criteria and reporting;
5. test closure activities.

Each stage represents a number of key tasks that need to be carried out in order to complete the formal testing as described in the ISTQB definition of UAT. The stages also represent the order in which these tasks are carried out, although we will see that in real life we will probably need to move between these stages, especially when additional functionality is identified that needs to be tested or faults are repaired that need to be retested. The FTP can be applied to any testing level or to an overall testing project.

For our UAT process we will add an additional stage at the beginning for the unique element of UAT of recruiting and forming a UAT team – unique because UAT is conducted by end-users rather than test professionals; it does not simply follow on as one more testing stage for the professional testers to do. UAT team recruitment, development and training are explained in Chapter 4.

The second stage aligns with the FTP's 'test planning and control' stage; it entails setting up the UAT project, identifying its purpose and goals, ensuring that we have a sound basis for testing, and planning all the remaining stages. The key input is requirements, which can be problematic, and Chapter 2 explains how we ensure we have the right requirements to work from. Chapter 6 explains in detail what we have to do at this stage.

The third stage aligns with the FTP's 'test analysis and design' stage; it entails generating tests from the requirements, using well-defined processes that we will explain in Chapter 3. The output from this step will be a complete set of tests that we need to implement to achieve our overall goal; this is explained in detail in Chapter 7.

The fourth stage aligns with the FTP's 'test implementation and execution' stage. At this point we need the system itself and any test environments needed to enable all the tests to be successfully executed. As we test we will generate data about the status of the system that we can report to stakeholders and we report any problems we find to the development team for investigation and, if appropriate, correction. This is explained in detail in Chapter 8.

Next comes a step that aligns with the FTP's 'evaluating exit criteria and reporting' stage. In our UAT process this is the point at which we gather together all the information from all the testing to determine whether the acceptance criteria have been met and, if not, how far short the system falls and what could be done about any problems. This vital information enables the final acceptance decision to be taken and guides the follow-up from UAT to system deployment. This is explained in detail in Chapter 9.

The final step aligns with the FTP's 'test closure activities' stage and extends it to consider the implications of what was found in UAT and what was decided about deployment. Valuable experience and knowledge gained in UAT can now be used to identify any 'workaround' solutions needed to overcome shortcomings of the system, guide end-user training and the user documentation needed to support users, shape the kind and level of technical support needed, and plan deployment mechanisms and timescales. This is all explained in Chapter 10.

THE MANY FACES OF UAT

Contract acceptance testing

Testing to determine whether contractual conditions have been met, so UAT is based on the requirements defined in the original contract for a system acquired from a third-party supplier.

Factory/site acceptance testing

For systems requiring installation after build, there may be a factory acceptance test to establish that the system meets requirements on completion of factory build before installation. Installation may have its own contractual conditions and there may be stage payments for completion of each stage, especially if installation involves shipping overseas. In this case factory acceptance will normally be based on requirements in the contract and site acceptance will be based on achieving the same set of requirements in an installed location.

Alpha/beta testing

When requirements are difficult to define or deliberately open-ended, a conventional contract acceptance may not be possible. In this case some form of 'testing in use' may be done. Alpha testing would be conducted at the developers' premises and beta testing would be at the customers' premises. The actual testing may be based on specific activities but more often is left to the users' discretion. For obvious reasons this is seldom used for custom-built systems, but may be used for releases of commercial products to the marketplace.

Field testing

Field testing is needed for systems that are deployed when in use, such as a control system for fire services. The system elements that are used in deployed locations are tested in their deployed environment to ensure that they are fit for purpose and sufficiently robust, and that communications with base facilities are effective.

FROM UAT TO SERVICE DELIVERY

The importance of testing throughout the development of an IS should not be underestimated and, as The Standish Group has shown, there is a strong argument for getting the eventual users involved as early as possible and for keeping them engaged throughout development. Some systems are built this way, but many more are not – and however we build a system, at some point it has to be transitioned from development to use. It is at this transition that most problems with a system become visible (though the root cause may have occurred much earlier). The choice is between unearthing the problems before and during the transition or living with them after the transition. Given that, for most systems, the transition involves some kind of handover from development to users that involves money or some other form of exchange, we need a mechanism for making the transition.

Figure 1.3 shows the transition phase at the end of development. It may have several steps, but UAT will be a critical step that will enable others. The transition may take many forms in different organisations and the UAT step will have to be shaped to the overall transition process, so UAT can also take many forms.

Figure 1.3 The transition to live use

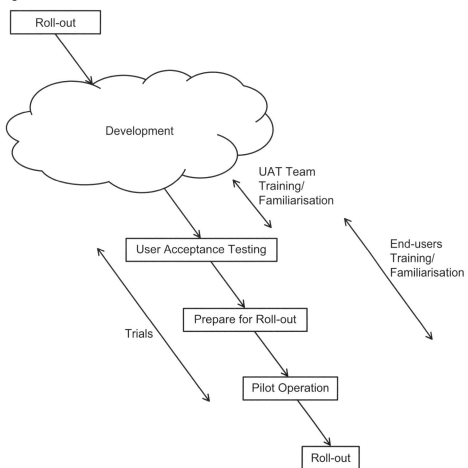

The tested system will then move on through other steps in transition that might involve running a pilot project to ensure that the system is capable of meeting the business need on a small scale before roll-out. At some point users will need training and familiarisation with the new system. Roll-out may need to be phased to reduce the impact on existing systems and processes. There may be many factors that can affect the transition mechanism, some of which are outlined below. The choice of transition mechanism will affect the nature of UAT and the way we plan it.

MANAGING THE TRANSITION TO LIVE USE

Pilot projects

A pilot project is a scaled-down implementation, usually in a controlled environment and with specially selected staff. The aim is to demonstrate that the system is ready for implementation and to identify any problems that might affect a full-scale roll-out.

Phased transitions

Following a successful pilot a phased roll-out can be used to gradually increase the scale of operations. The aim in this case is to provide an opportunity to confirm what was found in the pilot and to manage any issues that arise related to scale, for example logistics.

Training and familiarisation

All users will need training before roll-out is complete. This may be incremental with a phased implementation. Users will also need to become familiar with the system following training so that they do not lose the knowledge and skills acquired during training and so that they are reasonably proficient when the system goes into live operation. This is a separate exercise from UAT, although UAT will certainly enhance the system knowledge of the testers. If UAT is used for training or familiarisation, the effect is not only to slow down the testing but also to compromise the quality of testing because testers not trained on the system will be likely to make errors in designing and/or executing tests.

UAT AND CONTRACTS

In the development of an IS we typically see requirements evolve throughout development, so that the system delivered to UAT is typically rather different from that specified in the initial requirements specification.

Where a contractual agreement exists, however, the contract is normally based on an agreed requirements specification, and that specification will have been defined at the beginning of the contract and, therefore, also at the beginning of the project. Even if some allowances are made through the contractual mechanism for changes, it is almost inevitable that the contractual requirements (on which contractual acceptance must be based) will not completely describe the evolved business and user expectations at the end of the project. UAT must therefore embed contract acceptance within a wider UAT exercise.

We need to make a distinction between the acquisition of an IS and the development of an IS. We speak of developing an IS when we build the system in-house using our own resources so a contractual relationship is not necessary (although some organisations may use an internal contract to enable one part of the business to buy services from another). Even though the relationship between sponsor, business managers, end-users and developers may be relatively formal, the possibility of coming to a final agreement about what is an acceptable outcome always exists. If an IS is acquired from a third party, or if a third party is instrumental in developing and delivering it, the scope for flexibility in the end result is very limited.

FOUR WAYS TO ACQUIRE SOFTWARE FOR AN IS

There are at least four different ways we can acquire software:

1. Build the system in-house (with our own resources).
2. Outsource the development to a third party (who could be offshore).
3. Acquire a commercial off-the-shelf (COTS) solution configured to our specific needs.
4. License software for our use (software as a service).

An IS may use any of these to acquire the software part of the system and this will have an effect on how UAT is performed.

Build in-house

Within this category of systems, requirements may be documented before development begins or they may have evolved incrementally during development. In extreme cases, requirements may never have been documented at all or not documented in any detail. In all these cases some work will need to be done to match what has been captured in requirements with current user expectations.

The main advantage of building software in-house is that the key stakeholders – developers, sponsor(s), manager(s) and end-users – should all be available for consultation.

Outsource

A system acquired via outsourcing development will most likely have been designed and developed in a place remote from the location where it will be used. The requirements in this case may have been written by the acquirer, the developer or in some form of collaborative effort, but the likelihood is that they will be similar to the requirements we would get from an in-house development. The development process may also be similar to that used in-house.

Where the similarity ends is in the availability of information and the accessibility of key stakeholders. Sponsor, manager(s) and end-users should all be available, but developers will be off-site, making communication about requirements, testing and other aspects of the development activity more difficult. Essentially this acquisition is similar to in-house development but communication channels will be potentially less reliable, communication lines will typically be longer and information may be harder to get and take longer to acquire.

COTS

COTS software covers a wide range of systems from simple productivity tools to sophisticated decision support systems. COTS solutions are already defined and built in modular form so implementation involves selecting modules, configuring individual modules, where this is feasible, and installation. In this case there is no access to the requirements from which the modules were built and the purchaser (sponsor) must make any changes necessary to make the solution work by changing business processes.

UAT for a COTS system is, in some respects, very simple because the modules will typically be in use in other organisations and will have been in use for some time. There should be very few, if any, issues with the way the software functions. On the other hand, the fit with the business processes is likely to be less than ideal and assessing how well the solution will work in the business context and how well users will be able to adjust to its approach will be much larger concerns. UAT in this case is much more about assessing a solution than about testing software.

Software as a service

Software as a service (SaaS) may be used to provide services that the purchasing organisation does not wish to develop or host on its own systems. The service is provided under a licensing arrangement and is usually a 'standard' service that will be in use in many organisations; as a result, it should be stable and reliable in use. In some cases the service can be customised to generate changed or additional functionality to fit a particular business need.

In the case of SaaS solutions the main focus of UAT will need to be the fit of the solution to the organisation's business processes.

Whenever we do business with a third party we enter into some form of contract and, where a contract is in place, contract acceptance will be essential to enable completion of the contract and any payment associated with that event. However, contract acceptance does not fulfil all the objectives of UAT so we will need to ensure that UAT includes an agreed contract acceptance. That does not mean that UAT will be limited solely to contract acceptance; we will still need to plan to achieve all the other outcomes that give us benefits from UAT.

STAKEHOLDERS IN UAT

There are many stakeholders in an implementation, drawn from the business, its staff and its customers, the development organisation, any suppliers and potentially a host of others. In an ideal world all these stakeholders would be identified, consulted and informed of progress at every stage. In the real world this is hardly ever the case, but we still need to take account of the expressed needs of at least some stakeholders.

For the purposes of UAT the most important stakeholder groups will be:

- the sponsor, which means the person or group that commissioned the system (and defined the business intent);
- the manager(s) who will be responsible for delivering expected business benefits from the IS implementation;
- the end-user(s) who will actually operate the system;
- developers and other technical staff who are responsible for implementation and who will support the UAT effort.

Each of these stakeholder groups has a unique viewpoint that will influence UAT and each group has a set of responsibilities. Each group will be expected to deliver certain information and services and each will have information needs to enable it to carry out its role successfully.

Sponsors

The sponsor is the person who signs the cheques. In a small company the sponsor will typically be the owner; in a larger company a sponsor will typically be an executive at some level who has a budget to acquire software for the organisation. In both cases the sponsor's interest is in getting value for money by ensuring that the acquired software is fit for purpose, usable by the people for whom it has been acquired and meets the acceptance criteria.

The sponsor will normally initiate the risk analysis on which test prioritisation is based and subsequently be the person who makes the release decision. Unless the company is very small (sole trader or partnership), the sponsor is unlikely to be the user who will conduct the tests but may be involved in planning the UAT exercise.

The sponsor's main concern is with achieving the expected business benefits, so their focus of attention will be on identifying potential risks and barriers to success. Following risk analysis the sponsor will be most interested in defining test scenarios that will exercise the software in a realistic environment and take some measurements that give comfort in the performance of the software and its effectiveness in driving the key business success parameters, such as revenue, profit and cost.

Business managers

Business managers are those who will be commissioning the software and delivering the expected benefits so they will need reassurance that the software is usable and capable of achieving the claimed benefits. For this group the scope of interest is likely to be wider than simple fitness for purpose and the tests defined will need to enable the business processes designed around the software to be exercised by users in realistic scenarios. The scenarios will be based on the success criteria set by the sponsor and will ensure that users interact with the software and the business processes at a realistic level over a realistic time frame.

An example might be to carry out a few days' transactions, using saved data from real processing using the existing system, to ensure that the results are better than those achieved when the transactions were first exercised. This kind of exercise would need the original transaction details to be saved and stored, and it would need the complete system to be set up, with users suitably prepared, to repeat the set of transactions with the new system and measure the results. This is an exercise that may go beyond UAT but will necessarily include a UAT component that can be designed to achieve the desired test coverage and measure outcomes against acceptance criteria. The overall exercise, a form of trial or pilot, can achieve effective UAT as well as a benchmark of business performance for the new system.

There are also other management roles that will be involved in the UAT exercise. One of the most important of these may be a quality manager, who would be primarily interested in the overall quality of the delivered system, or a test manager, who would be responsible for the overall quality and effectiveness of testing and would advise and guide the UAT team to enable them to achieve the best possible UAT with the resources available.

End-users

End-users are those who will directly interact with the system, either inside the organisation (staff) or outside the organisation (suppliers and customers). So a group of end-users is not necessarily a homogeneous group with a single set of expectations; there may be multiple viewpoints and sets of expectations to be satisfied. Since end-users directly interact with the system it is clearly appropriate for this group to carry out the actual testing at the user interface and a team made up of as many end-user viewpoints as possible should be formed for that purpose. The primary role of this team will be to assist in designing the tests and then to execute them and report on the results. A vital secondary role, however, is to raise any issues or insights that arise as they carry out the tests so that the user perception of the system is as fully explored and documented as possible.

For end-users the nature of testing will be in a practical context, so test cases should replicate realistic scenarios and use realistic data to enable the testers to operate the software as it will be utilised to achieve the IS's overall purpose.

End-users of software may be drawn from any specialism or none. They may have lots of previous computer experience or none. Their common characteristic is that they will be expected to use the new system to achieve their own business targets. Depending on the level of previous experience with computers and especially with systems of the kind being tested, users can be encouraged to identify scenarios that will entail use of the software to achieve a particular business outcome. Those with significant experience will be able to suggest scenarios of interest in testing, such as those that will be particularly challenging for the system, those that will be particularly prone to errors and those that will involve high levels of user interaction. These scenarios will ensure that the testing is based on real business activity, while other tests can be defined to provide adequate test coverage and ensure that all the higher risk areas of operation are adequately exercised.

While end-users are expected to make up the body of a UAT team, it is important that business managers and sponsors are aware that the UAT exercise should also involve exercising their expected interaction with the system. In a well-balanced UAT team all three roles will have some part to play directly in the UAT exercise, but even if this is not possible the dependencies between the roles need to be well understood.

Developers and technical support staff

Although the developers' main work should be completed by the time UAT begins and the work of technical support will not yet have started in earnest, these two groups can make a vital contribution to successful UAT. Developers have an important role in helping UA testers to gain familiarisation with the built system and they will be assessing any incident reports raised during UAT to determine what remedial work may be required. Getting this work done promptly can have a significant impact on the time it takes to complete UAT. Technical support staff will be responsible for managing any test environments put in place for UAT and for keeping the system under test in a serviceable and usable condition. Without them the whole exercise could grind to a halt before it gets properly started.

CHAPTER SUMMARY

The main purpose of this chapter was to provide an overall view of what UAT is about at the broadest level. It has provided a basic understanding of what UAT is and outlined its unique role and purpose in preparation for the content covered in the rest of the book.

The definition of UAT identified the need for formal testing and the importance of acceptance criteria and of understanding the users' real needs rather than relying on a specification written at the beginning of the development project. The basic concept of the business requirement has been introduced and this will be expanded in Chapter 2, but we need to remember that business requirements represent the reason a system is being constructed and this may be quite different to what was originally captured in the requirements specification.

We have shown where UAT fits into the overall process of implementing ISs, where UAT fits into the sequence of testing (regardless of the model the project follows), who carries out UAT and whose needs are primarily considered during UAT. We have also identified how UAT may be affected by the way a system has been built or acquired.

We have considered the evidence that ISs often fail at introduction or after change and we have examined the characteristics of ISs that make them vulnerable to potential mishaps. An analysis of the CHAOS report provides surprising and interesting information about how closely ISs reflect the original business requirements, and important conclusions can be drawn about the value of keeping stakeholders involved throughout the development process.

The way UAT is carried out to avoid damaging failures represents UAT as a form of risk management, and UAT also has an important role to play in building user confidence, assessing the readiness of the system for deployment, and preparing for roll-out.

Finally we have identified the key stakeholders in UAT and their roles and we have outlined the main areas of cost associated with UAT.

After reading Chapter 1 you should understand the purpose and the benefits of UAT, and who is involved in UAT, and understand and justify its costs.

What have you learned?

Test your knowledge of Chapter 1 by answering the following questions. The correct answers can be found in Appendix B.

1. In what way does UAT differ from other testing carried out during development?
   - **A.** UAT takes longer to do than other kinds of testing
   - **B.** UAT must be carried out by end-users
   - **C.** UAT evaluates the system against the requirements specification
   - **D.** UAT can be informal testing as long as it is done by users

2. Which **three** of the following are used as the basis of UAT?
   - **A.** Technical specifications
   - **B.** User needs
   - **C.** Requirements specification
   - **D.** Acceptance criteria
   - **E.** Business processes
   - **F.** Tests developed for system testing
   - **G.** Automated tests designed by the developers

3. Why is it vital for users to carry out UAT? Select **three** options.
   - **A.** Because they have more time available than developers and testers
   - **B.** Because they are not experts on the technical performance of the system
   - **C.** Because the users' ability to use the system as a tool to achieve business benefit is critical to success
   - **D.** Because only users will be able to recognise some situations in which the system's behaviour may be counterproductive
   - **E.** Because developer testing has less value than UAT
   - **F.** Because the system must be evaluated against user needs and use actual business processes.

Some questions to consider (our responses are in Appendix B)

1. What questions would you ask if your organisation asked you to carry out UAT on a new piece of software that is being introduced to support the sales activity in your business?

2. How would you react if your boss told you that the development project for which you will be doing UAT is running late and he wants you to do UAT in parallel with the developers completing the development?

3. Why not just get professional testers to do UAT? After all they have experience of formal testing and know all the techniques.

2 BUSINESS REQUIREMENTS

Now that we understand the context and purpose of UAT the next stage is to understand the business requirements. This chapter explains what requirements are, how requirements are written and how the business requirements relate to UAT. It will also become clear why requirements may be out of sync with the real business requirements by the time UAT takes place and how this limitation can be overcome.

Topics covered in this chapter

- Business requirements
- Business intent and user expectations
- Acceptance criteria
- The requirement types
- Prioritising business requirements
- The relationship between business requirements and UAT
- The relationship between development and UAT
- Scope of UAT
- Building a UA test basis

BUSINESS REQUIREMENTS

In Chapter 1 the fit between an IS and its business users was referred to as being like the fit of a garment that is 'made to measure'. Using the same analogy a requirement identifies something that the customer wants to specify about the item of clothing about to be made for them. Similarly, a business requirement is something a business wants to specify about the IS it is about to have built or is about to acquire. In other words a requirement is simply something that we need and in the context of an IS, a requirement is something we need from the system. The better the desired outcomes and the detail of what the system ought to do is understood, the better the chance of delivering what is needed. Requirements describe what a system ought to do, what will be built and what will be tested during UAT.

Having captured the needs of the organisation the project team will document them in a requirements document using clear and simple language and using the terminology of the user. These requirements, if too general to be of use to developers, can then be translated into a more technical version using a structure aimed at helping the development team to understand and build the system. The resulting document is known as a requirements specification (RS) and the detailed needs of the business contained in it are the requirements.

UNDERSTANDING THE SYNTAX OF REQUIREMENTS

What do requirements look like?

Requirements can be expressed in many different ways and they do not all look the same. Requirements may be recorded in a document, in a spreadsheet or in software designed specifically for recording requirements.

Here are some simple examples of requirements but bear in mind that any requirements document you are given for UAT may contain much more than this very basic information.

Example 2.1

Table 2.1 Business requirements

CR1	An administrator is able to add a new user
CR2	An administrator is able to adjust existing user details
DB1	The system supports that 100 previous versions of a contract are available in a version history

As long as the language and terminology used is familiar to the people who requested it and to those who will develop it, then these are good examples of what requirements ought to be; namely a clear description of a requirement of the system.

However you may find that the requirements document you have been given contains much more than just this very basic information.

Example 2.2

These requirements, related to the security of a website, were entered into a system as opposed to written in a document. As well as a description of the requirements this document also contains some other valuable information.

Table 2.2 The requirements document

Project	Reference	Category	Description	Priority	Current status	Actions
UNT v0.2	S_01	Security	Users will be able to change their own password	1	None	Edit/Delete
UNT v0.2	S_01.1	Security	There will be an option for users to change their password on the main menu	3	None	Edit/Delete
UNT v0.2	S_01.2	Security	There will be an option from the login page for users to request a password reset if they have forgotten their password	3	None	Edit/Delete

The name of the project
This field may not be needed where a requirements document relates to one project only; however, it may be relevant to software that can record requirements related to multiple projects.

A unique identifier of the requirement
Every requirement should have a unique identifier, which ensures that any further project documentation that is created can refer back to which requirement an activity or line item relates to. Because the purpose of the project is to meet the business requirements, the unique identifier is one of the cornerstones of all the project documentation that follows the RS. Note that there is a difference between the unique identifiers in the two examples above.

In the second example you can see that there are two different IDs that split the requirements into one larger overall requirement (S_01), and the detailed requirements that belong to it (S_01.1 and S_01.2), whereas there is just one level of ID in the first example (CR1).

The category
It probably makes sense for most RS documents to group together requirements in categories that cover similar ground. These categories cover any related parts of the functionality that the project is delivering and can be logically grouped together under headings such as: 'Creating a contract', 'Invoicing', 'Proposal maintenance', 'Workflow' or

'User interface design'. Categories may include functional aspects of the system – what it ought to do – as well as non-functional aspects – how it does what it ought to do. The non-functional requirements may be written by the project team if they were not requested by the business and cover topics such as the speed and usability of the system.

The priority
It is useful in most, if not all, cases to understand the priority of a requirement as it will help to schedule the development work and prioritise testing. In theory it is possible to use any scale; however, it is quite common to use 'critical' and 'non-critical', or to use a scale of 1–3 or 1–5, 1 being the highest priority and 3 or 5 being less important. The assumption made when writing the RS is that all the requirements are needed – hence the name 'requirement' – but that some are more critical than others.

Current status
It may or may not be important to track in the requirements document whether the requirement has simply been requested or whether it has been built or tested. If it is important, a status field or column can be created for the purpose in the RS.

Edit/Delete
In the example for project UNT v.02, the system that the requirements are logged on keeps track of the version history of requirements and the Edit/Delete buttons allow users of the document to make changes to the requirements. This may not be relevant in your case; however, it is useful to remember that requirements can, and often do, change. The RS should be revisited and reviewed during its life in order to make sure that the documented requirements still reflect what is happening on the project and what the current business needs are.

Exercise 2.1

The case study we will use throughout the text is of an accounting system named Excelsior, which has been created to deal with the accounting-related processes such as purchase orders, contracts and payments. It also has a number of modules that allow staff to carry out HR-related tasks. HR details can be updated and

Table 2.3 Excelsior requirement

Key	Name and description	Rank	Priority	Assigned to	Status
Request saving and background updating					
BW4	The system will allow saved requests to be automatically updated	34.0	High	Nobody	In progress
	Once a request has been saved, users will receive request updates when and if they become available				

requests can be made for other changes such as absence, training or expenses. What information can you glean from the following business requirement?

The answer can be found in Appendix B.

Please note that if you are asked to review a requirements document or specification and you do not understand the requirements in that document, you may need to ask some questions of those that do.

BUSINESS INTENT AND USER EXPECTATIONS

We established that requirements are gathered and documented in a business requirements document, a set of statements that describes all of what a user community wants from the IS. The requirements as a whole should reflect the overall objectives and expectations of the business. These overall objectives and expectations, although they are often forgotten, should also be documented.

Every IS is created for a purpose: to achieve some business benefit such as improved productivity for staff or reduced costs of operation. The purpose of the system is usually called its 'business intent'. Business intent is important because it identifies what the business is expecting to be able to achieve when it has the system installed and operating.

Arising from the business intent the sponsor, managers and end-users will have a perception about what the system should do and how it should behave. Users of systems already in place will also have expectations based on their perception of the way they currently work and the way they are expecting to work with the system. Expectations may not be exactly aligned with business intent but they are an important element of perceived success, so they should be captured as an input to UAT.

A key driver of success in IS implementation is the transparency of business intent and user expectations so that all stakeholders, including the developers, have a common understanding of what is required and what is expected in an IS solution. The absence of effective transparency is a key risk factor because the parties may be operating from different assumptions, and UAT is the final opportunity to identify and resolve any misunderstandings that may have arisen during development. If the business requirements match the business intent and the system meets the business requirements, the business intent will have been achieved.

Example 2.3 – Business intent

- The system will enable the business to manage 250 customer accounts simultaneously.
- The system will enhance throughput of widgets by 10 per cent.
- The system will enable the business to offer five new services.
- The system will enable the business to deliver customer orders within 48 hours of order.

The business intent should be measurable and immediate. Once the system is installed it will be possible to determine if the business intent has been achieved, so it is also feasible to test for achievement of the business intent at UAT. A more strategic long-term objective, such as reducing staff numbers for example, cannot be tested at UAT. For this reason it is preferable to base the achievement of longer-term objectives on improvements that can be seen and verified immediately.

EXERCISE 2.2 – BUSINESS INTENT

For the project you are currently involved in, or for a previous project, list the overall goals that make up the business intent from memory or, if no business intent was written, from your knowledge of the project:

- _____
- _____
- _____
- _____

Were you able to list the overall goals? Were they specific enough to be measurable?

Unless the stakeholders, managers, developers and testers are aware of the overall requirements the IS must meet and understand how they should be measured, it will be harder to meet those goals. Whether or not the goals were met is an essential ingredient of UAT. The ability to decide together, based on an agreed measure, whether the project has been a success or not and whether the system should be accepted is what UAT should be able to achieve.

ACCEPTANCE CRITERIA

Before we look in more detail at the requirements and the different requirement types, we should examine the acceptance criteria.

Acceptance criteria

The exit criteria that a component or system must satisfy in order to be accepted by a user, customer or other authorized entity. (ISTQB Glossary)

The business requirements tell us what the system must do for the business so we will base our tests on them. Acceptance criteria, on the other hand, tell us how we will know that the system is fit for release to its users. In other words acceptance criteria are our way of determining when we have done enough testing.

Example: at least 90 per cent of all business requirements must be tested.

This acceptance criterion prevents a scenario in which only a small sample of requirements end up being tested. Acceptance criteria can be quality-related as well as system-related. For example we would not want a system released if all requirements had been tested and all the tests had failed. We can guard against this eventuality by imposing quality-related criteria.

Example: there must be no critical defects outstanding at release.

Acceptance criteria are the conditions that must be satisfied before a system can be accepted by the users or stakeholders. Accurately defining the acceptance criteria is one of the most important elements of a successful development project and clear acceptance criteria are critical to the success of testing. Inaccurate or incomplete acceptance criteria can lead to low customer satisfaction levels, missed deadlines and increased development costs.

The fact that all documented requirements should be met would be an implicit acceptance criterion, although it could also be stated explicitly. Other criteria would extend this to define the status of the system when it is offered for release. Examples might be:

- All requirements shall be tested before release.
- There shall be no critical defects and not more than two high-priority defects outstanding on completion of acceptance.
- There shall be no unallocated incident reports outstanding.

These three criteria should ensure that what is released is complete and in a stable state, which is clearly important for the user population.

Acceptance criteria have another useful purpose. If, at the scheduled release date, the acceptance criteria have not all been met, they can be used to provide a measure of outstanding work and the possible delay if the system is held until all criteria are met.

For example if a system has one critical defect and four high-priority defects outstanding, we can discover relatively easily how long it will take to clear the defects and retest to ensure the fixes are correct. This provides a measure of possible delay. We could also consider whether the effects of any of the outstanding defects could be mitigated by some kind of 'workaround'. Acceptance criteria set up a dialogue between UAT, developers, users and sponsor through which a release date acceptable to all can be negotiated.

THE REQUIREMENT TYPES

So far we have identified that the RS is a document, usually written by a business analyst or a developer, which defines the business requirements in a form that developers can understand and respond to. However, the requirements are not homogenous and we can identify different types of requirements: functional requirements, informational requirements, behavioural requirements and environmental requirements. The RS should ideally contain all the different types of business requirements as well as expressing business intent, capturing user expectations and defining acceptance criteria.

Business requirement types

All business requirements contain information about what the business wants the new system to do, but there are different types of business requirements that we can distinguish between. In many organisations only two requirement types are used: functional and non-functional requirements, but there are at least four distinguishable types of business requirements:

- functional requirements;
- informational requirements;
- behavioural requirements;
- environmental requirements.

Functional requirements

Functional requirements are the type we are already familiar with, in that they define what the system must do. Functional requirements cover business processes that could be independent from technology, for instance 'purchase order sign-off' or 'shipment', and as a result are often easiest to understand and define. The system will apply logic to an input and produce the required output. On the basis of functional requirements the development team will build the parts of the IS that the end-user interacts with.

Example: the system shall validate that all passwords have a mixture of upper- and lower-case characters and at least one number.

Informational requirements

Informational requirements define the information provided to the end-users to help them do their work. They also cover to what extent information sharing and access control are required and set out the requirements for the information that is generated as input data, output data and stored data for the processes defined in the functional requirements. Some additional data and metadata that are technology-related rather than process-related may also be defined as part of the informational requirements.

Example: customer account files shall contain the fields: CustID, CustName, OrdDate, OrdQty and OrdPrice.

Behavioural requirements

Behavioural requirements describe how the solution has to act. They are often called non-functional requirements and they can be defined quantitatively or qualitatively.

Example: a qualitative behavioural requirement might be that the user interface must be user-friendly. This can be made verifiable in a number of ways: by relating it to existing standards, for example the Microsoft UX Guide, which is a guide to user experience interactions; or by defining parameters of the user interface, such as the number of colours used and the allowable uses for each colour.

Quantitative measures easily translate into numbers but qualitative behavioural requirements also need to be translated into a quantitative measure. The user interface requirement that covers the responsiveness of the system, for example, will have to be quantified in a way that can be measured and tested.

Example: response time for recalling customer address details will not exceed 1.5 seconds.

Environmental requirements

Environmental requirements, sometimes referred to as 'constraints', describe the context within which the IS will operate. This may include where each component of the IS is to be physically or geographically located, any industry standards to which it must adhere and any constraints on the use of technology; for example the system must be accessible from platforms running MS Windows, Unix or Linux. They should also cover any regulatory restrictions.

Many of the requirements in the last three categories, the non-functional requirements, are less likely to be requested or written by stakeholders and more likely to be added by the project team. Although the requirements do describe the needs and wants of the business, a lot of other information represented in the RS is often of a much more technical and abstract nature.

In practice a RS may not contain all of the information we need and the translation from business-speak to developer-speak that we mentioned earlier may have 'blurred' some aspects of the business requirements. Worst of all, the RS may have to be written and approved before development can begin so that it represents a snapshot of what the business requirements were believed to be at the beginning of development.

We will, in all probability, need to supplement the RS before we can plan, design and run effective UAT and we will see how we do that in Chapter 6. For now we will work on the basis that whatever documentation we have is an adequate expression of business requirements.

PRIORITISING BUSINESS REQUIREMENTS

Neither time nor resources are unlimited for UAT so tests probably have to be prioritised in some way that balances the expectations of each stakeholder group. Prioritisation also ensures that if time runs out, everyone can feel reassured that the most important (highest priority) aspects of the system have been tested.

Sponsors will naturally be most concerned about the business intent so a way to express the intent is needed, and business criticality is one way to determine which aspects should be tested first. Similarly users and managers will have concerns about how the system operates so their concerns will be encapsulated in the idea of usability.

Business criticality

Business criticality is a measure of how important any individual requirement is to the success of the business or to the achievement of the business intent. We could define any number of levels from absolutely critical to not at all critical, but what is usually done is to define just two – critical and non-critical. Within these two broad categories priorities are then attached to each individual requirement (or possibly to groups of related requirements) to enable the organisation to prioritise development and plan accordingly. For UAT we can use the same measures of criticality and priority to manage the UAT priorities or, if priorities have not already been assigned to requirements, we can consult the sponsor to determine the criticality for testing.

Usability

Usability has a technical meaning that gives rise to a specific type of testing known as usability testing. For UAT we have neither the expertise nor the time or resources to do usability testing in a rigorous way, but we do have a set of expectations that we can use to determine some simple parameters for testing. For example if the sponsor has an expectation that the system will be able to handle 30 specific transactions per hour then managers will have an expectation that the throughput of a single terminal multiplied by the number of terminals will at least equal the required throughput of transactions, while the end-users will want to satisfy themselves that the user interface at any single terminal will enable them to handle the expected number of transactions overall.

For each requirement or group of requirements the business criticality can be used to generate a priority for testing and the usability criteria for those requirements acquire the same level of prioritisation.

Business process

The definition of UAT included testing the system according to 'user needs' and 'business processes'. We will need at least some of our tests to exercise business processes so this will be a third focus for our prioritisation of requirements for testing; we will group together aspects of the system related to specific business processes and test them together so that we can determine whether the system correctly implements the business process.

THE RELATIONSHIP BETWEEN BUSINESS REQUIREMENTS AND UAT

The RS is the document we usually see as the point of contact between users, developers and testers. It is intended to express to developers what the users want so they can build the system, and simultaneously to express to the UA testers what the users want so they can test the system independently of the developers. The word 'independent' is very important here; it is the key characteristic of UAT.

UAT is an expression of the RS (as interpreted by UA testers); the system itself is an expression of the RS (as interpreted by the developers). Comparing these two expressions by running the UA tests is the only way we can determine whether the outcome of development matches what the users said they wanted. So it is absolutely vital that UA testers work independently of the developers in designing their tests and it is equally vital that they work from an expression of the requirements that has not already been interpreted by the developers; otherwise UAT would simply reflect the developers' interpretation.

We have shown previously that, although it should be the embodiment of what the business wants and needs, the RS may be out of date, incomplete or inappropriate because:

- The needs of the business were not documented in detail (or at all).
- The needs of the business changed during the development project and the RS has not been kept up to date.
- The documentation was deliberately written only in outline at the outset and was then developed iteratively and incrementally.

These situations are all likely to lead to a state of affairs at the end of development in which the delivered system is not aligned with (current) user expectations. In addition to the fact that the RS may not be completely accurate, further mistakes may have occurred down the line. The problem that sponsors, managers, end-users and developers have in describing what an IS must do is that the sponsors understand the business background but (usually) not the technology; users and managers understand what the system is meant to do but (usually) not how it will work; while the developers understand the technology but (usually) not the business background. A middle ground is hard to find because the four stakeholder groups use different ways to communicate and have different views of the world. What is usually done is to try to define the business need in terms the users understand and then 'translate' it into 'technology speak'.

This process can cause problems for two very important reasons:

- Translations are never simple or completely accurate, so the translation process introduces errors.
- Both groups have a set of information that, as far as they are concerned, 'everybody knows'. These assumptions are seldom stated in requirements because the author's mindset does not recognise any gap in the information. Meanwhile readers take what is written literally and try to deliver it according to their own assumptions. This is a major source of serious requirements gaps.

So an RS is likely to be a flawed expression of business requirements, especially if it is drafted and approved at the start of the project. In addition:

- Requirements defined at the beginning of a project may contain errors and/or omissions that need to be corrected.
- Users may gain new insights during development that lead to requirements changes.
- The business environment may change in a way that forces requirements to change (for example in a system related to taxation there may be revisions to taxation law).

We will therefore need to assess the RS and, if necessary, update the requirements as expressed in the RS at the end of the project and document these as a basis for testing.

THE RELATIONSHIP BETWEEN DEVELOPMENT AND UAT

There are many ways to develop software but most fall into three broad categories: sequential development, iterative development and component-based development.

Sequential development

Sequential development uses a sequence of development stages that typically follow a V shape as shown in Figure 2.1. Discovering and documenting initial requirements is the first stage in this process and UAT is the final stage. The approach breaks a system down into manageable chunks and functionality is not normally delivered until the end of the project.

Figure 2.1 A sequential development life cycle

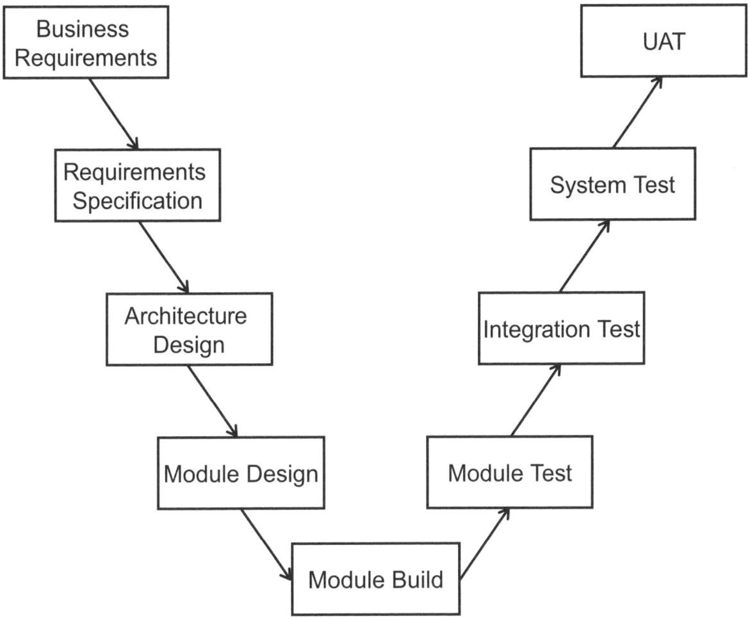

Notice that the test levels relate to different stages of design in which the requirements are analysed and then broken down into smaller and smaller building blocks. The test levels then test the outcomes of each of these design stages. UAT is the final test level that tests the completed system against the requirements.

Iterative development

In an iterative approach (such as agile development) the design and testing takes place during short development 'sprints' so that system functionality becomes available incrementally at the end of each sprint (Figure 2.2). In this case requirements are implemented incrementally according to a plan, but not all requirements are documented initially. UAT will be required before roll-out to confirm that the system is acceptable, but there will be no requirements documentation to form a test basis.

Figure 2.2 An iterative development life cycle

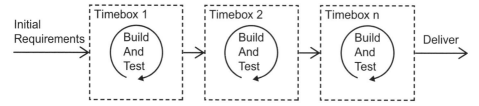

Component-based development

Other common ways to develop systems build on one or other of these fundamental models. For example a system can be constructed from commercially available components integrated into an architecture that meets the business requirements. In a component-based system architecture the component 'building blocks' are likely to be well defined but the integration will involve greater risk. UAT should encounter relatively few problems with the way the system functions but problems can occur, for example where integration of components does not deliver exactly what was required. A related approach, using COTS software, acquires most of the functionality in a collection of existing modules; development involves configuring the modules to meet the business requirements. In this case much of the focus of UAT will need to be on whether the solution is a good fit with business intent.

SCOPE OF UAT

The scope of UAT is defined in the UAT plan and is of vital importance to its success. It defines the extent of UAT: what will and what will not be tested. Clearly the requirements will be tested but the scope explains the extent of the deliverables and the boundaries, including those things that are out of scope. We saw earlier that within this parameter we have to ensure that the most critical requirements are tested first according to the perspectives of the most important interested parties. But are there any additional things we should test or definitely should not test?

What we must test

Firstly one thing that is not negotiable is the testing of contractual requirements. If the system is being delivered in fulfilment of a contract, then we must carry out contract acceptance testing to ensure that the delivered system meets all the requirements stated in the contract. Even in this case, though, there are likely to have been variations, some documented and some not, that will need to be taken into account.

Secondly we have to aim to test the business intent and user expectations by prioritising requirements and usability according to the business criticality of each requirement. This must include anything explicitly mentioned as a deliverable in a contract and anything explicitly defined in the RS.

Thirdly we need to ensure that we test every business process from end to end. Business processes have not been tested prior to, and must form the framework for, UAT. Any functional requirements should be tested as part of the known existing or future processes as requirements that do not relate to business processes may not be relevant in the new system.

Fourthly we must test any defect fixes that are outstanding and any fixes for defects that we find.

Finally we must carry out a regression test for every change that occurs. Regression testing checks whether the defect has been fixed and confirms that the fix has not caused any other problems.

What we will not test

With the limitations of time and resources we have already mentioned, it would clearly be impossible to test everything about the IS, but then many aspects will already have been tested. Unit testing (testing the code), integration testing (testing whether parts of the code or system work together) and system testing (testing whether each part of the system functions correctly) have already been carried out, and repeating any of these tests is outside the scope of UAT.

So UAT will not test anything that has already been tested in one of the development testing phases (provided we have evidence of the tests) and, in particular, it will not set out to test all of the functions of the software.

For reasons stated earlier we will not attempt to test usability in detail; nor will we attempt to test performance, except that we will embed some usability and basic performance measurements in business process testing.

ARIANE 5 – THE IMPORTANCE OF SCOPE

On 4 June 1996 the unmanned rocket Ariane 5, built to launch satellites for communications, earth observation and scientific research, was launched. It exploded just 40 seconds after lift-off on its first voyage after a decade of development costing £4.5 billion. The Ariane 5's cargo was valued at an additional £324 million. The cause of the failure was a software error in the inertial reference system (SRI – derived from the French equivalent of the name), the navigation system that calculates the position, orientation and velocity of the rocket during take-off. The SRI had been designed with a backup so that when the on-board computer (OBC) detected a critical issue the backup SRI would take over. Unfortunately the main SRI and the backup SRI contained the same error (an internal SRI software exception was caused during data conversion where the number that was converted had a value greater than what could be represented in the converted value format). This resulted in an operand error causing both SRIs to fail. The complete loss of guidance meant that the launcher veered off its flight path, broke up and exploded.

The inquiry board in the official report on the causes of the disaster stated that:

Testing at equipment level was in the case of the SRI conducted rigorously with regard to all environmental factors and in fact beyond what was expected for Ariane 5. However, no test was performed to verify that the SRI would behave correctly when being subjected to the countdown and flight time sequence and the trajectory of Ariane 5. It should be noted that for reasons of physical law, it is not feasible to test the SRI as a 'black box' in the flight environment, unless one makes a completely realistic flight test, but it is possible to do ground testing by injecting simulated accelerometric signals in accordance with predicted flight parameters, while also using a turntable to simulate launcher angular movements. Had such a test been performed by the supplier or as part of the acceptance test, the failure mechanism would have been exposed.

The scope, or what is included in the requirements and thereby in UAT, is key to the success of an implementation. It is easy to make assumptions about what ought to be included based on what has worked well previously or how a requirement ought to be tested. The scope must be viewed in light of the current project, making as few assumptions as possible, and a culture should be encouraged where project team and stakeholders feel collectively responsible for the content of the IS and the extent of the testing, and empowered to speak up if anything seems to have been omitted.

BUILDING A TEST BASIS FOR UAT

Test basis

All documents from which the requirements of a component or system can be inferred. The documentation on which the test cases are based. If a document can be amended only by way of a formal amendment procedure, then the test basis is called a frozen test basis.

The life cycle of an IS begins with identifying and documenting business requirements, which then become the basis for development. In theory, then, we can use the requirements documentation as a basis for our UAT. In reality, however, this is not always the case, so we need a foolproof way of defining a test basis for UAT that does not rely on a complete set of initial requirements. The key sentence in the definition of a test basis (see box) is the second one: 'The documentation on which the test cases are based.' We need a test basis for UAT as a set of documents and what we have at present is an RS. In some situations we will have to test strictly against the original requirements; for example if a contract for development was based on them. In most cases we need to extend the information in the RS.

Evaluating/enhancing the RS

The requirements as a whole and each individual requirement need to be checked to ensure that they are of the required quality. If stakeholders are unfamiliar with how business requirements are formulated they may make their requirements too:

- high level;
- ambiguous;
- focused on the solution instead of the business need;
- general and not focused enough on specific user groups;
- all-encompassing, lumping together multiple requirements.

Requirements are checked and updated by reviewing them as a team of interested parties and stakeholders. Members of the team may also individually review the document with a checklist (containing the characteristics of good requirements for example) to note any comments and questions before a walk-through takes place. Review techniques will be explained in more detail in Chapter 3.

CHARACTERISTICS OF GOOD REQUIREMENTS

Gathering requirements is an imperfect process and mistakes will occur. Very few people have been trained how to elicit, analyse and document quality requirements and the RS may contain many badly written requirements. So what should we look out for when reviewing a requirements document? Here are some key things to consider.

Ambiguity

A good requirement is unambiguous. The reader should only be able to interpret the requirement in one way and draw one conclusion. The requirement should contain no jargon or ambiguous language such as 'fast', 'user-friendly', 'several' or 'efficient'.

Mistakes

A good requirement should be correct. Only the user representatives can identify whether the requirement reflects what they intended. The end-users or other appointed stakeholders should sign off or otherwise agree that the document accurately reflects their needs.

Feasibility

A good requirement is achievable. Good requirements must be implementable within the project's technological, budget and resource restrictions. This is not directly UAT's concern, but any infeasible requirements will raise questions about what was actually implemented, and these need to be explored.

Necessity

A good requirement is needed. A requirement should meet a genuine need of the business and should have been requested or agreed to by someone with the appropriate level of authority.

Priority

A good requirement is prioritised. Especially for the purposes of UAT, a key part of risk management is to test the highest-priority requirements first. Without priorities UAT becomes much more difficult to manage.

Verifiable

A good requirement can be tested. A requirement should contain a concrete quantitative measure that can be tested even when covering requirements related to quality.

GOOD AND BAD REQUIREMENTS

Bad examples:

- 'The website must be user-friendly and fast' (too high level and contains two requirements). What exactly is meant by user-friendly and how would we test this? What would happen if we found it to be user-friendly, but not fast? Would it fail our test or pass?
- 'All documents must be branded' (ambiguous). What kind of branding? What are the documents involved?
- 'We need visibility of what contracts are about to expire' (not thinking in terms of user groups). Does this affect every user or only a specific user group?
- 'An email must be sent automatically on enquiry' (focusing on the solution instead of the business need). Is email the right answer? Perhaps the real requirement is that the customer be notified? The correct answer may be by email, fax, letter or SMS based on their preference. What if the enquiry did not come in via email?

Good examples:

- The design should be simple enough so that users will be proficient to use the IS after a day's training.
- All non-managerial sales staff need to be able to see which of their contracts will be expiring within the next three months.
- The IS should be accessible from Internet Explorer and Google Chrome.
- Contracts should open in less than 0.5 seconds.

If a UAT team works from the requirements as originally documented, the UAT exercise is likely to hit all sorts of problems. Our review of the RS may discover some of the problems, but it cannot solve them and we will need to be sure that we test thoroughly in areas where we believe the requirements were flawed. If we find requirements gaps we can still go back to the users to supplement the RS by revisiting business intent, user expectations and business processes. With these three sources brought up to date we should be able to form a test basis.

Our next step is to look at these additional sources to find a way of enhancing what we have in the RS.

Capturing the business intent

If the business intent is not already documented, has not been documented well or has changed, the first step will be to discuss and document the business intent with the stakeholders. The business intent represents the overall goal of introducing the IS and is a great first step in creating the test basis because it gives UAT a very clear focus on what is needed. The business intent, like the requirements, must be clear, unambiguous and measurable.

Capturing user expectations

We can capture user expectations by talking to users. Our conversations can be helped and supported, though, by a simple technique known as 'user stories'. We can ask users to write down, or help us to write down, user stories that encapsulate their expectations.

User stories

A user story is a very brief description of what the system does for its users to help them perform their work more easily. User stories are used in agile development 'to facilitate the discussion and support planning' (Adzic, 2009: 160). They are a valuable tool for us because they avoid any details of specific requirements or of how they might be implemented. They simply provide a very brief and simple expression of user expectations.

A typical user story is made up of one or two sentences in the everyday language of the end-user that covers what a user needs to do as part of their job function. One common format is to use the formula 'as a …….. I want ……. so that …….'. This gives a clear link to expected benefits without asking users to articulate any details of specific requirements and is ideal for our purposes.

Example 2.4

As a team member I want to be able to complete a draft contract so that it can be processed.

As a manager, I want to be able to approve a contract created by my team.

The 'three Cs of user stories' (http://www.xprogramming.com/xpmag/expCardConversationConfirmation.htm) provide a good practical basis for capturing and exploring user expectations.

Card
User stories can be written on small index cards; small enough to capture the key idea and not large enough for a complete requirement. The cards can then be used as tokens for discussion.

Conversation
The conversations related to user stories can explore the relationships between stories and, if necessary, add detail for clarification.

Confirmation
Each user story must be verifiable so that we have a way of knowing whether it has been correctly implemented or not.

An exercise in collecting, documenting and discussing user stories can add not only a clear idea of what user expectations are, but also a means of identifying the results we would expect to get from a test based on each user story. This is exactly what we need.

Capturing business processes

We will need to review the business processes and check that they interface correctly with the requirements, for instance that the requirements contain all the functions and accept inputs as defined by the business processes. If necessary we may have to supplement them. We will describe the review technique in greater detail in Chapter 3.

Where business processes interface with the computer we can use the concept of use cases to capture what the software should do for each user activity and then compare that with the RS.

Use cases

Use case

A sequence of transactions in a dialogue between an actor and a component or system with a tangible result, where an actor can be a user or anything that can exchange information with the system.

The definition (see box) describes precisely what we are looking for. It involves a dialogue between an actor and the system that makes up a sequence of transactions with a tangible result. An actor is a representative of some role (such as an end-user who is making a purchase or an end-user who is completing an order); the transactions are the actions accomplished by the system for the actor. So here we have a description of how a user role would interact with the system to achieve some goal (such as placing an order).

As well as actors, use cases are normally associated with scenarios, where a scenario is a sequence of steps representing one specific action. In our case we can build a scenario for the 'normal' process, meaning the scenario in which everything works correctly and the process completes successfully. We can then add supplementary scenarios to explore the 'error' cases, for example where the process diverges from the 'normal' case in some way.

Use cases can be expressed in simple diagrammatic form or as a sequence of numbered steps. For our purposes the latter is probably the better option so that users can work with us as we build out the use cases that represent the business processes and their interactions with the system.

Table 2.4 Use case

Book cruise

1.	The agent suggests a travel option for the client
2.	The system searches for date options according to the criteria and the suitable options are listed for the agent
3.	The agent chooses Select Holiday
4.	The system verifies there are cabins available and reserves a cabin
5.	The agent supplies payment details to finalise the booking
6.	The system books the cabin and issues the ticket

Alternatives

4a.	Cabin is not available in the desired class
	4a1. The system informs the agent that no cabins are available according to the price criteria
	4a2. The agent specifies another price range
4b.	Cabin is not available at all
	4b1. The system informs the agent that the cruise is fully booked
	4b2. The agent specifies another cruise

Example 2.5

In this use case the actor role is the travel agent (an end-user of the system who uses it to sell holidays). The alternative scenario explores what happens when no suitable cabins are available.

This is a simple use case but it is easy to identify business process steps not involving system interaction (step 1) and system interactions (steps 2–6). The interactions can be described in more or less detail, as can the parts of the business process not involving the system. Use cases are potentially much more detailed than user stories and are normally aimed at providing developers with complete requirements.

If use cases have been used in capturing the initial requirements we gain the benefits for very little additional effort. If not, use cases provide one of the simplest and quickest ways to capture key information.

We will see how we can deploy user stories and use cases in setting up a UA test basis in Chapter 6.

CHAPTER SUMMARY

In this chapter we have looked at what business requirements are and how we capture them for the developers and for UAT. We also learned that, in addition to the detailed requirements, the business intent and user expectations ought to be documented so that these three aspects together meet both the goals and expectations of the business.

We learned that there are different types of requirements and the RS contains more than just the requirements. We recognised a number of pitfalls that can cause problems and a number of reasons why requirements, however good initially, rarely make it to the end of a project without becoming out of date. The test basis is created to overcome these issues, producing a valid and up-to-date document from which to generate tests.

Techniques such as user stories and use cases enable us to enhance the RS to provide a current and reasonably complete test basis for UAT.

What have you learned?

Test your knowledge of Chapter 2 by answering the following questions. The correct answers can be found in Appendix B.

1. How could you best define the business intent?

    A. The main reason for and benefit of the new system

    B. The reason for carrying out UAT

    C. The expectations users have of how the system will work

    D. The purpose of the business

2. What are business requirements?

    A. A strategy for UAT

    B. The test basis

    C. A set of statements that describe what the system ought to do

    D. Both (b) and (c) are true

3. What is a limitation of requirements?

    A. No requirements may be recorded

    B. Things have changed since the requirements were written

    C. The requirements may not be recorded in enough detail

    D. All of the above are true

4. Which of the following is a characteristic of an unsuitable requirement?

    A. Too much detail

    B. Too high level

    C. Not technical enough

    D. Focused on the business need not the solution

Some questions to consider (our responses are in Appendix B)

1. You are a stakeholder new to the project and are asked to read the RS to get an idea of what the project is about, but you do not understand some, most or all of the requirements. What would you do?

2. What is the difference between an RS and a UA test basis?

3 TESTING BASICS FOR UAT

We know from the definition of UAT that the tests we design need to be formal so we need to know how to test formally, even though we will be aiming to generate simple tests based on our common-sense understanding of what the users' needs are. We will also need a range of different kinds of tests to cover all the aspects of UAT, so we will need a range of design techniques.

In this chapter we will build the testing toolkit that we will need so that we can use it effectively when we come to construct the tests for UAT. As we do this we will explain the key terms you need to be aware of and the basic processes, and then we will go on to build a few simple tests as a way of practising the skills.

Topics covered in this chapter

- What is testing?
- Test types
- Testing processes
- Test-case design techniques
- Testing approaches for UAT
- Reviews

WHAT IS TESTING?

What does the word 'testing' conjure up? It might be the image of the dummies used in testing cars to destruction to ensure they are safe to drive, or the kind of rudimentary checks we might do on a spreadsheet we built to use in the office, or the more rigorous testing that professional developers do to ensure their code works before they hand it over. None of these describes the kind of testing we need to do for UAT.

What we need for UAT is a 'formal' kind of testing that will enable us to check that a system does everything it is supposed to do and nothing that it is not supposed to do. We may be accepting something very expensive that should transform our business but, if there are any problems, could damage it. Testing of this kind is serious stuff; it needs to be robust, reliable and rigorous. That is why we opt for formal testing.

Formal testing

Testing is an objective and structured evaluation of a system (or a piece of software) against a standard. Evaluation must be objective rather than subjective so that we can be confident that the results of testing can be relied upon; testing must determine absolutely whether a piece of software meets its specification (the standard) or not. There is no room for personal opinion, judgement or guesswork. Testing needs to be structured so that we can be sure that we have evaluated the system against the requirements completely, in the sense that every requirement has been tested at least once. A structured approach enables us to ensure that every requirement has at least one test.

Also, if we assume that any defects and deficiencies discovered during testing will need to be corrected, testing must also provide objective evidence of what is wrong with the system so that the development team can quickly and accurately identify the sources of defects or deficiencies and correct them. This is another aspect of a structured evaluation.

Testing contrasts with activities like debugging, which are designed to find and eliminate defects during the development phase. In debugging a developer picks inputs that they think might break the system so that they can remove the defects. In effect, because the developer is both the expert and the fixer of bugs at this stage, they can do testing and bug fixes themselves. In UAT, as in all formal testing, the testing and bug-fixing activities are deliberately kept separate. The end-user can find but not fix errors, and the developers can fix errors but not carry out the testing.

The primary objective of UAT is to tell us what the status of a system or a piece of software is, in particular (in our case) whether it is fit for release. To do this testing must be:

- systematic, so we know exactly what has been tested and what has not;
- derived from the specification of what the system is supposed to do, so we can ensure everything that needs to be tested actually gets tested;
- repeatable, so that if we find defects we know the development team can repeat our test and get the same results to help them locate the defect;
- documented, so we can evaluate the quality of the tests.

Testing comes in many shapes and sizes, but all formal testing conforms to these same criteria. These are the characteristics UAT has in common with other types of software testing, but UAT is also unique in some respects.

Test levels

In Chapter 2 we looked at a life cycle for software development called the V life cycle. In that life cycle we have several stages of testing, which are called test levels (because they test software as the system is built up, level by level, from individual units of code). Each test level has its own unique set of objectives.

For example at the unit test level we would look for evidence that the unit functions correctly, at the integration test level we would look for evidence that units can communicate and function together, and at the system test level we would look for evidence that the whole system works as specified.

Each test level is a formal test based on the specification at that level, so unit testing would be based on the unit specifications and so on. The relevant specifications are therefore called the test basis for that level.

At every test level we may have many different aspects of the software or system to consider such as functionality, reliability, usability, security and so on. Each aspect of the system that we test will need its own specific test type. Functional testing is designed to test that functionality at a given level is correct with respect to the test basis. Security testing is designed to test that security requirements have been met at a given level and so on.

UAT is the highest test level because it represents the level at which requirements were formulated. Every level below UAT should have been tested before UAT begins, so UAT is the final check that what has been built meets the requirements of the end-users and sponsor.

TEST TYPES

Test type

A group of test activities aimed at testing a component or system focused on a specific test objective, which means functional test, usability test, regression test and so on. A test type may take place on one or more test levels or test phases.

Of all the test types that might be defined, two are particularly useful for UAT: functional testing and structural testing.

Functional testing

Functional testing is exactly what it says: testing that required functions are present and that they work correctly.

Functional testing

Testing based on an analysis of the specification of the functionality of a component or system. This is also commonly known as black-box testing.

Functional test design technique

A procedure to derive or select test cases based on an analysis of the specification of the functionality of a component or system without reference to its internal structure.

We have to analyse the business requirements to identify all the functional requirements, define test conditions and generate test cases for them. Figure 3.1 shows what a functional test looks like.

Figure 3.1 Functional testing

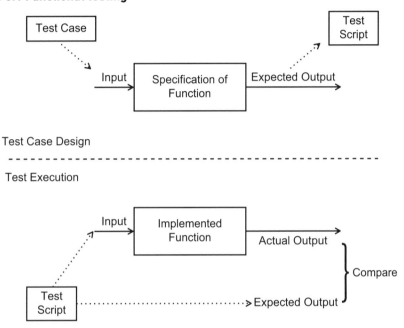

In Figure 3.1 a functional test case has been created from a test condition. The input data specified in the test case are then applied to the specification of the function to be tested (in the business requirements or in a more detailed specification if one exists) to discover what output(s) that input should generate. These are all recorded in the test script.

When the test is executed the test script is used to identify the required data input and this time the actual output(s) are recorded in the test script. The actual and expected outputs can then be compared to determine whether the test has passed or failed.

The vast majority of test scripts generated for UAT will be functional.

Structural or white-box testing

Structural testing

Structural (white-box) testing is based on an analysis of the internal structure of the component or system.

59

White-box testing is most often associated with testing code, but it is useful for testing anything that has internal structure. In UAT we need to test system components such as menu structures and we also need to ensure that the system operates correctly with business processes. We can utilise white-box testing in these cases to explore the relevant structures and to ensure that we exercise all of the possible routes through the structure (a form of (structural) test coverage).

If we take a business process as an example, we know that each path through the business process will trigger one or more use cases that will exercise system functions and generate outputs. The business process may then utilise the outputs in some way.

This is an example of end-to-end testing if we initiate the business process to generate inputs to the system and consume outputs from the system. Successful completion of the business process indicates a successful end-to-end test case and within that test case a functional test case will have been utilised to transform data.

Example 3.1

Figure 3.2 shows a simple business process that has three paths corresponding to the responses to the two questions embedded in the process. If the answer to 'Existing Customer?' is 'Yes', the process moves to the next question 'New Account Type?' If this too is a 'Yes', the process requires two actions: 'Generate Authority' and 'Send to Customer' (path 3). Each of these activities will have a use case from which we can generate functional test cases. So an end-to-end test of path 3 involves a user operating a business process using the system and completing that process via two test cases and probably a manual activity to generate a mailing to a customer. The process flows from its beginning to its end.

If we follow the same testing approach for paths 1 and 2, we will have completed the entire business process; that is we will have achieved 100 per cent structural coverage of the business process, utilising some existing test cases along the way.

A LITTLE QUALITY EXPERIMENT

Imagine we have a system with 100 requirements and we give three testers the task of testing it as well as they can. Tester 1 runs 100 tests, tester 2 runs 200 tests and tester 3 runs 1,000 tests. Which tester did the most effective testing?

The answer is that we cannot tell. Although tester 3 ran the most tests, we cannot be sure what was tested so we do not actually know how effective the tests were.

If we specified that every requirement must be tested at least once and we repeated the exercise, the results would be rather different. Tester 1 runs 100 tests, tester 2 runs 200 tests and tester 3 runs 1,000 tests. There is no change except that all three testers now claim that all requirements have been tested. What can we conclude?

If tester 1 has covered every requirement, then that set of tests must be more efficient than the other two testers' tests because it achieved the same result with less effort. But we still do not know whether the three sets of tests were equally effective. The moral of the story is that more does not necessarily mean better and test effectiveness needs to be based on some other criterion. That criterion is called coverage.

Coverage is a measure of exactly what parts of a system are tested by each individual test. If we can demonstrate (this will need some documentation) that our tests have been designed so that every requirement has been tested at least once, then we have achieved 100 per cent requirements coverage and the smallest set of tests that achieves 100 per cent coverage is the most efficient.

Incidentally the documentation of the tests also enables us to check that the tests work. Around 10 per cent of test failures are typically caused by defects in the test rather than defects in the system, so it is worth checking the tests before we run them.

Figure 3.2 Business process end-to-end testing

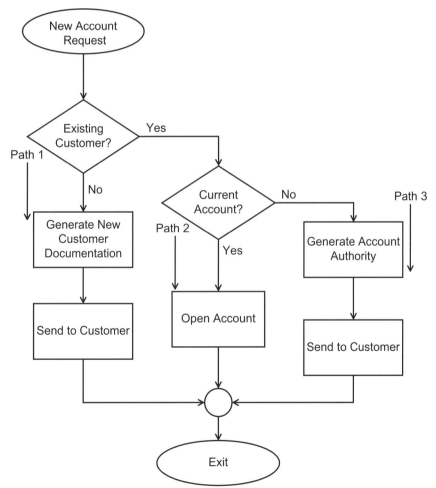

In UAT we look especially for business requirements coverage. If we specify 100 per cent test coverage, we mean that every single requirement has one or more tests defined and when those tests are executed we can be certain that 100 per cent of the requirements have been tested. We will later introduce test-case design techniques that enable us to achieve desired levels of test coverage and also test our system efficiently, in the sense that we will use the minimum of time and resources to achieve a given level of test coverage – the Holy Grail of testing.

Bear in mind, though, that one test may not be enough to test a requirement completely, so 100 per cent requirements coverage may mean that every requirement has been subjected to at least one test. If we want to be more thorough (perhaps for the more critical requirements) we may have to design more than one test for some requirements and adjust our coverage measure accordingly.

One question that we will have to wrestle with continuously is, 'What exactly are the business requirements?' We need a test basis for UAT and we know that the initial RS is unlikely to be an adequate test basis. We will return to address that problem when we come to planning the UAT exercise.

TESTING PROCESSES

We want to be able to complete UAT in the most efficient and timely way we can. To do that we need two key processes: the FTP, which will help us to ensure we do the right things at the right time, and the test development process, which will be used to ensure we design the right kinds of tests so we get a clear answer to whether the system meets the business requirements and the acceptance criteria.

The fundamental test process

As we defined in Chapter 1, the fundamental test process (FTP) has five steps:

1. test planning, monitoring and control;
2. test analysis and design;
3. test implementation and execution;
4. evaluating exit criteria and reporting;
5. test closure activities.

We will use this simple process to structure the step-by-step guidance in Chapters 6–10. It gives us the sequence of activities we will need to follow to achieve our objective and also provides useful pointers to the kinds of outputs we might need to enable us to make a rational decision about acceptance at the end.

The test development process

The test development process (TDP) describes the mechanism for generating effective tests that achieve a required level of test coverage. The process comes in three stages, each of which is aligned with a step in the FTP.

The TDP has three components: test conditions, tests cases and test scripts. These are all defined in the ISTQB Glossary and reproduced in the box below.

Test condition

An item or event of a component or system that could be verified by one or more test cases, e.g. a function, transaction, feature, quality attribute, or structural element.

Test case

A set of input values, execution preconditions, expected results and execution post-conditions, developed for a particular objective or test condition, such as to exercise a particular program path or to verify compliance with a specific requirement.

Test procedure specification

A document specifying a sequence of actions for the execution of a test. Also known as test script or manual test script.

Test condition

The purpose of a test condition is to express some aspect of the business requirements (a function, transaction, feature, quality attribute or structural element) in a form from which a specific test or tests can be constructed. A test condition can be either **true** or **false** and the value of the test condition can be determined by running a test case.

Example 3.2
If a feature describes secure login to a system using a username and password, there are a number of test conditions that can be written:

1.   If a valid username is entered with the correct password, the user is logged in to the system.
2.   If a valid username is entered with an incorrect password, an error message appears.
3.   If a non-valid username is entered with a password, an error message appears.

There are other test conditions that could be written in addition to the above three, depending on the requirements of the business.

Notice that each test condition represents a single component of the feature that can be assessed as either true or false. The feature is correctly implemented if and only if all three conditions are true.

For each test condition we could construct a table to identify what the test condition means as follows.

Table 3.1 Test conditions table

Valid username	TRUE	TRUE	FALSE	FALSE
Correct password	TRUE	FALSE	TRUE	FALSE
User logged in	TRUE	FALSE	FALSE	FALSE

Each entry in the table can now be tested with a test case that evaluates to TRUE or FALSE.

Test case

We need to identify inputs and expected outputs associated with each test condition so that we can generate specific tests to determine whether the test condition is true.

Preconditions and post-conditions identify the state the system must be in before the test is executed and the state it will be in after test execution respectively.

One or more test cases can be written for each test condition.

Example 3.3
Here is a set of test cases written for the first test condition from Example 3.2.

Test condition 1: If a valid username is entered with the correct password, the user is logged into the system.

Table 3.2 Test cases

Test Case 1	Precondition	User not logged in
	Inputs	Valid username
		Valid password
	Outputs	None
	Post-condition	User logged in
Test Case 2	Precondition	User not logged in
	Inputs	Valid username
		Non-valid password
	Outputs	Error message
	Post-condition	User not logged in
Test Case 3	Precondition	User not logged in
	Inputs	Non-valid username
		Valid password
	Outputs	Error message
	Post-condition	User not logged in
Test Case 4	Precondition	User not logged in
	Inputs	Non-valid username
		Non-valid password
	Outputs	Error message
	Post-condition	User not logged in

Preconditions and post-conditions are useful for sequencing tests, for example if a precondition of a test is that the user is already logged in to the system, it would make sense to ensure it is not run before the test case concerned with logging in to the system.

When a list of all the possible test conditions is written, it may be that some of the test conditions are duplicates. If the outcome (logging in) is dependent on there being both a valid username and a matching valid password, then you could argue that test case 3 and 4 are duplicates because a non-valid username will not allow the end-user to log in, regardless of whether they have a valid or non-valid password. In fact you could argue that a non-valid username cannot have a valid password. However, in our example we want to test that the combinations of the different valid and non-valid entries produce the required outcome. For test case 3 we can enter a valid username that contains an error with the corresponding valid password. Test case 4 can test the equivalent of a hacker trying to gain access to the system by entering a random invalid username and password.

Test script (test procedure specification)

Test scripts provide the mechanism and documentation to run the tests we have defined as test cases. A test case is generic; it defines the nature of input and expected outputs, and provides a template for constructing test scripts with actual data. UA testers need to be armed with a collection of test scripts that they execute in a particular sequence.

In Example 3.2 we have defined a template for successful logins. We could use that template to generate a test script that, for example, logs in 10 valid users (particularly useful if we have a way of automating the input). More interesting, though, is that we could define a test script to exercise test cases associated with all four test conditions and then run that script with a mixture of valid and non-valid usernames and valid and non-valid passwords.

Example 3.4
Here is a simple test script that corresponds to test case 1 above.

Table 3.3 Test script

Login1: Normal user login

Purpose	Users are able to log in with an acceptable user ID and password
Preconditions	User is not logged into the system. Test account has been set up successfully
Test data	User ID: tester1@acme.com
	Password: UAT1
Process steps	1. Click system icon
	2. Enter user ID
	3. Enter password
	4. Click Login

Table 3.3 (Continued)

Login1: Normal user login

Result	User is logged into the system on the Home page
Post test	User tester1@acme.com is logged in
Notes	

Note that this simple test script can be extended to log in multiple users and extended to include the other test cases.

Example 3.5 – A more extensive test script
This is a test script to test a specific test case uniquely identified as test case 4.11.

4.11 Test script 17 – Check the functionality on the login screen

4.11.1 Test conditions:

1. Check end-users can log on to the system with a valid user ID and password.
2. Check end-users cannot log on to the system with an invalid user ID.
3. Check end-users cannot log on to the system with an invalid password.

Test # 1 – Check the end-user can log on to the system with a valid user ID and password.

Test step	Test description	Expected results	Pass/Fail comments and observation numbers raised
Scenario 1 – Logged out of the system on the start menu			
This scenario tests: • A valid user ID and password.			
Expected results: • The end-user is successfully logged on to the system.			
1.	Click the system icon	The login page is displayed. The following fields should be displayed and should be blank: • Username • Password	

(Continued)

Test step	Test description	Expected results	Pass/Fail comments and observation numbers raised
2.	Enter tester1@acme.com in the User ID field	The username should be displayed in the field	
3.	Enter UAT1 in the password field	A * character should be displayed for each character of the password	
4.	Click the login button	The homepage should appear and the username should be displayed in the top right corner of the page	

Note that the terms used in our (real) example are different from the terminology used in this book. In the example the test script is what we have referred to as a scenario and vice versa. This is a very common occurrence in UAT and as long as all the stages that need to be delivered are understood and the term universally used, it is less important that those stages are known by a different name in your organisation. Note also that the script only has three test conditions because in this instance the condition that tests a non-valid username and non-valid password was deemed unnecessary.

Each script contains: test-case number and version, test description, requirement number, tester, process step numbers, process step descriptions, test data to be utilised, expected results, error descriptions, pass/fail results, date tested and comments from the UA tester. The following are the elements that should be included in addition to the above in a scenario containing multiple test scripts:

- scenario name and number;
- scenario description;
- test script names, numbers, versions and dates;
- IDs of the test cases and requirements covered by the test script;
- description of the test cases;
- any prerequisite procedures.

Numbering test scripts is part of the traceability of the test documentation. It serves to measure how many test scripts, test cases, requirements and acceptance criteria have been covered during UAT. Test scripts can also be reused with updated version numbers and dates for the purposes of regression testing.

Test coverage

As we explained earlier, test coverage is an important measure of how much testing has been done.

If a requirement generates 50 test conditions, then those 50 test conditions need to be evaluated to achieve 100 per cent coverage. If 100 tests are run but only one of them relates to a test condition, then only two per cent (1 out of 50) coverage has been achieved. The way test coverage is measured differs from one test-case design technique to another, but in every case the test coverage measure compares the number of tests carried out so far with the number of tests that are possible on the software under test using the given technique. Test coverage is our objective measure of how much testing has been done and therefore how comprehensive the UAT's outcomes are.

A UA test design plan requires a collection of test conditions to be extracted from the requirements to achieve whatever level of test coverage has been specified for the tests. From these a set of test cases is generated that defines all the inputs and expected outputs for all of the tests, and finally a set of test scripts is created that will enable UA testers to execute all the tests and record the results.

Example 3.6
For the login example (3.2) above, based on the assumption that conditions 3 and 4 are not duplicates, the test condition generates four test cases, all of which are needed to completely evaluate the test condition. Each of the four tests would carry 25 per cent of the coverage for that particular requirement and all four would need to be run to provide 100 per cent coverage of the requirement.

TEST-CASE DESIGN TECHNIQUES

Test-case design techniques exist for a wide variety of different approaches to testing a software object, many of which are described in Hambling et al. (2010). Any of these can be used to design test cases and some will certainly improve overall productivity, especially if they are easy to understand and use.

Equivalence partitioning (EP) and boundary value analysis (BVA)

EP and BVA are two related test-case design techniques that are invaluable in the UAT context. Despite the long and technical-sounding names these are very simple and intuitive techniques to use, so it is well worth getting familiar with them.

EP helps to understand what values should be used when data values are in a continuous range, such as all the integers between 1 and 10. It provides a simple way to give us confidence that the system correctly handles all the values within the range, so it gives us efficient yet complete testing.

Here is a simple example. If a data entry field for a surname can contain up to 50 alphabetic characters, there is no benefit in testing all the different combinations of alphabetic characters that can make up a name. We could not even if we wanted to – the number of possible combinations of 50 alphabetic characters is astronomical, and that only accounts for the valid examples.

EP allows us to assume that any valid combination will behave like any other valid combination – so we only need to test one example to give us reasonable confidence that the system will accept any valid combination of characters. We call that very large collection of possible inputs the valid partition. Within this partition any valid combination of characters will demonstrate that data entry will work and therefore represents one valid test case. In this equivalence class, entering 25 valid characters would be as valid a test as entering any other valid combination of characters fewer than 51 characters long, and only one would need to be tested. Note that we have chosen to use the middle of the partition for our valid case in this example.

If there is a valid partition there will also be at least one invalid partition. In fact there are three different invalid partitions that we have to take account of in this case:

1. any combination of 1–50 characters that contains at least one invalid character (for example a numeric character);
2. combinations that contain fewer than one character (which means no characters);
3. combinations that contain more than 50 valid characters.

We will need one example of each of those to make up a complete set of tests of the equivalence partitions.

You need to be aware that EP only saves us time and effort when the inputs are structured into lists, sequences or other collections. It is a limitation, but not that much of a limitation because input data fields are usually structured.

BVA is a natural partner for EP. BVA takes account of the observed characteristic that more application errors occur at boundaries or edges of data than anywhere else. Developers commonly process structured data with loops, and an error in entering or terminating a loop will cause a problem at a boundary (for example the first or last item to be processed in a sequence). It is also true that 'edge cases' are those we often get wrong in business processes, so developers may be working from an incorrectly specified boundary value to begin with. For these reasons boundary cases are great places to go looking for problems.

BVA exploits these observations by clustering tests at boundaries, and one good thing about partitions is that they invariably have boundaries. In our EP example above the boundaries are combinations of 1 character and 50 characters. For our purposes in UAT we can test the actual boundary values and one value just outside each boundary. The term 'just outside' means outside by the smallest possible amount in the situation. In our case the character combinations can only increase or decrease in length by one, so 'just outside' is one outside.

Applying BVA to our example would then lead to the following test cases:

1. two values at the boundaries for the positive values: 1 character and 50 characters;
2. two values just outside the boundaries: 0 characters and 51 characters.

You may recall that we already selected a test case with zero characters so we do not need to repeat that. Now the notion of using a value in the middle of the partition as the valid value makes sense; we are going to test at the edges anyway.

We have now whittled down an astronomical set of possible tests to just four tests: an input of 25 valid characters, an input of 25 characters with one or more of them invalid, an empty input field and an input of 51 valid characters. This saving of effort comes with no compromise on the quality of the testing.

There are many other test-case design techniques that you can explore, but EP and BVA on their own will give us plenty of support for the kind of tests we will need to run.

TESTING APPROACHES FOR UAT

We mentioned earlier that UAT is unique in some respects. The uniqueness arises from the U in UAT. UAT is uniquely driven by end-users (or those who will become end-users of the system once it is implemented). In other words the testers are not expected to be software or testing professionals and there is no expectation that they will have any experience of testing. In fact the reverse is true; the end-users' distance from the development specialism and relative closeness to the business specialism give them a unique perspective that is not influenced by what was built or how it was built. Only end-users can be objective in this context and, since they will ultimately operate the system, any intuition or experience they can bring to the exercise will add value.

One other thing makes UAT unique. Unlike all other kinds of testing, which are based on testing outcomes against a specification, UAT is based on three elements:

1. business requirements;
2. business processes;
3. user expectations.

We could argue that business requirements are documented in a specification (the RS) but, as we have already seen, the RS is not necessarily a valid basis for testing. We might also argue that business processes are specified, but that is not always the case. User expectations are not only not documented, they are also subject to change as the users gain experience.

So we need an approach to testing that mirrors these three elements.

Requirements-based test cases

Test cases must cover the business requirements because the requirements are what UAT sets out to test. In order to show that the requirements-based test cases relate to a specific requirement, the test case should contain an ID that links it to a business requirement. There is one layer of complexity that we should add at this point to do with the timing of test design. So far we have made the assumption that the test cases are created at the end of the project as part of the UAT preparation. However, you may find that the test cases were written shortly after the RS and that the existing test cases are out of date and must be updated according to the newly reviewed RS. The disadvantage of using requirements-driven test cases is therefore that if the requirements contain mistakes, the test cases will also be wrong.

Business process-based test cases

Business process-based test cases are test cases written to help make sure that the system that is delivered will work specifically in supporting the business processes. The test cases must be able to show that the requirements have been met in a way that reflects how the organisation is going to use the system. For business process-based testing, the tests must be sequenced to reflect the processes in order to check that they reflect the paths through those processes.

We showed in Example 3.1 how structure-based testing can be used to achieve coverage of business processes.

User interface-driven test cases

User interface-driven test cases are structured around forms or screens that need to be completed. Test cases are based on data entry, interactions via the screen and reporting. In each case these will be related through a scenario so that data are manipulated in a realistic way. User interface-based test cases can be embedded within business process-based test cases where the business process involves data entry, interaction or reporting. User interface testing might include:

1. Tab order – is the tab order correct?
2. Required fields – are the required fields marked and is an entry required?
3. Data-type errors – can the data only be entered in the correct format (dates, numeric, currency)?
4. Save and delete confirmations – does the system prompt the user to save changed data before closing and confirm a delete?
5. Shortcuts – do the shortcuts work?
6. Invalid menu items – are any menu items shown that are not available for the context users are currently in?
7. Links – do links work?
8. Menus – do the correct menu items appear?

Setting priorities – risk-based testing

One final aspect of testing for UAT is that we will be doing it under time pressure because we do our testing just before the system is released. If the system is late reaching the UAT stage we will be under even more pressure. In recognition of that we need a way of doing the best we can with the limited time available. For this we use a prioritisation mechanism that ensures we run the most important tests first, so that any testing that cannot be completed is guaranteed to be less important than the testing we have already done. We call this risk-based testing.

If we have an understanding of what aspects of the system are most important and might cause a serious problem if they were not effective, that is they represent risk, we can prioritise tests by risk level and test the highest risk areas first. We can begin by identifying the risk level for each requirement or group of requirements and putting them in priority order. That is at least a practical starting point for developing test cases. Risk-based testing can be used in conjunction with other approaches. For example we can apply requirements-based testing as a way of achieving requirements coverage and then apply risk-based testing within the requirements-based tests to ensure we test the most important areas first.

One final thought on test approach

Although we are interested in whether the software works or not, the developers and testers will already have tested this; specifically whether the software performs according to the technical specification. Our concern is not about compliance with the technical specification. If the system does what we want and need it to do while missing some detailed part of the technical specification then that will be an outcome that we should report, but it may not be something that, for us, is a 'show-stopper'. If, on the other hand, the system met every single item of the technical specification and the RS, but we found it to be cumbersome in use or it failed to support key business processes, then we would have cause for concern.

That is the nature of the end-user perception. We test to ensure we get what we need, even if that is not what was specified. The customer is always right.

REVIEWS

One further testing technique that we will need to be familiar with is the technique of reviewing.

Review

A review is an evaluation of a product or project status to ascertain discrepancies from planned results and to recommend improvements. Examples include management review, informal review, technical review, inspection and walk-through.

As the definition indicates, there are many kinds of review but the purpose is always the same: to evaluate and improve. We will use reviews as a key tool for evaluating and improving RS and test conditions, test cases and test scripts. We will concentrate on a very simple and informal kind of review, a variant of the walk-through mentioned in the definition, which will use the following basic process:

- Read the document individually and identify any problems or questions.
- Meet with the author of the document and other reviewers so that the author can 'walk through' the document and answer any questions.
- Capture any unresolved questions or problems in a document to give to the author after the review.

The evaluation is achieved by each reviewer contributing comments to enable the author to identify things that need to be changed or corrected; the improvements come from the changes the author will make following the review meeting.

Reviews provide benefits to a team over and above the improvements to documents that can be made. For example:

- Reviews are a team event so they help with the process of team building and getting to know each other.

- All participants are aware of the status of the reviewed document and the improvements made so reviews help to keep everyone involved and informed.

- The opportunity to ask questions of the document's author offers learning opportunities so that team members can build their knowledge of the system and the tests.

- Responsibility for the quality of the reviewed document is shared so everyone has a stake in quality.

- There is an opportunity to learn from more experienced colleagues so knowledge and experience can be pooled effectively in the team.

We will introduce a walk-through into the planning stage of UAT preparation by reviewing the RS in Chapter 6.

CHAPTER SUMMARY

This chapter has introduced some key testing processes and techniques for generating effective test cases, demonstrating how they can be adapted and focused on the specific needs of UAT.

Reviews in general, and the walk-through technique in particular, have been introduced as a valuable technique for evaluating and improving documents and also contributing to the team's development.

After reading this chapter you should be able to answer the following questions:

- What steps do I have to follow to ensure my UAT is complete?

- What steps do I have to follow to build an effective set of tests for UAT?

- How can I use reviews to ensure the documentation I have acquired is fit for purpose as a test basis?

- What techniques are available and how should I use them?

What have you learned?

Test your knowledge of Chapter 3 by answering the following questions. The correct answers can be found in Appendix B.

1. Which of the following best describes test coverage?

    A. Test coverage is the ratio of functions tested to the total functions

    B. Test coverage is a count of the number of tests that have been run

    C. Test coverage is a measure of the number of different things tested by a test

    D. Test coverage is the scope of testing

2. Which of the following is a benefit of using reviews to evaluate documents?

    A. Reviews give testers the opportunity to criticise developers' work

    B. Reviews are inexpensive to perform

    C. Reviews find all the defects in a document

    D. Reviews encourage teams to work together

3. What does the BVA test-case design technique test?

    A. BVA tests that users cannot enter non-valid data

    B. BVA tests that a system recognises whether data are within a specified range

    C. BVA analyses how the system performs when it is subjected to extreme conditions

    D. BVA generates test cases that should all fail

Some questions to consider (our responses are in Appendix B)

1. Your organisation is reluctant to allow UA testers to be part of a review process. What would be the best way to overcome that reluctance?

2. You are being offered a training course before starting work as a UA tester. What would be your requirements for a one-day course? Suppose you could have three days of training. What changes would you make to your requirements?

4   THE UAT TEAM

In Chapter 1 the concept of stakeholders, each with a different role to play in an implementation, was introduced. The sponsor commissions the system and signs the cheques, the manager is responsible for delivering the benefits of the system, the end-user operates the system and the developer builds the system. Each role has a different contribution to make to the project and each role has different objectives. UAT represents the first time that all the roles will potentially reach a moment of resolution regarding their own goals and responsibilities. The sponsor will know whether the cheque should be signed, the manager will know whether the business benefits will be delivered, the end-users will know whether the system works in the way they had envisaged and the development team will know whether its development work has met the requirements.

In this chapter we look more closely at the testing team and its relationship with other stakeholders. The mechanics of team formation are well known, but the UAT team has a unique challenge – to acquire the skills it needs, to form an effective team quickly and then to take on a challenging task and complete it in a very short time.

Topics covered in this chapter

- Stakeholders and the UAT team
- Key roles in a UAT team
- Creating a successful team
- Training the team
- UAT training content
- The team life cycle
- Dealing with team conflict
- The working environment and working patterns
- Basic disciplines

STAKEHOLDERS AND THE UAT TEAM

Not all of the people interested in UAT are considered to be part of the UAT team, yet some will have an influence over how it is conducted. These are stakeholders in UAT, even if they are not considered as stakeholders of the system being delivered. Depending on the scale of the project and the organisation they might include:

- programme manager – responsible for delivering a number of related projects;
- project manager – responsible for delivering the project;
- project management office (PMO) or administrative staff – responsible for organising UAT;
- test/quality manager – responsible for all testing including UAT;
- UAT team leader/manager – responsible for delivering UAT;
- UAT trainer – responsible for delivering UAT training;
- business analysts – responsible for documenting requirements.

The UAT team's primary responsibility is to provide the key stakeholders with enough information to make a rational decision about whether or not to accept the system. Evidence will be based on a programme of structured testing to determine the achievement of acceptance criteria. It is the UAT team's responsibility to plan, schedule, execute and report on the testing to provide stakeholders with detailed evidence and a recommendation (for acceptance or non-acceptance) based on that evidence. The stakeholders will also require recommendations about potential alternatives, for example to accept the system subject to receiving an update that corrects known defects within an agreed time frame.

The UAT team

The ISTQB Glossary does not include an entry for 'UAT team', but normally when people refer to a UAT team they mean those actively taking part in the UAT process; the UAT team leader or manager, possibly business analysts and the UA testers. UAT teams vary widely in their size and composition and the team may only comprise a single individual, but coordination, analysis and testing still need to be carried out and having specialists in these roles can help to make UAT more effective and efficient. Where the team is relatively large, that is more than three people, additional specialist roles can be identified.

We always need to bear in mind that the members of the UAT team may have other responsibilities in their day-to-day working lives or on the project. Not everyone will be available continuously or full-time, especially in the preparation stages, and work schedules will need to take account of availability as well as recognising that UAT team members may have to deal with other priorities in their other roles during the period of UAT. It is true that a dedicated team with no distractions can do the best job, but that is a situation that only rarely happens and we would be unwise to assume it in our planning.

According to Wikipedia:

A team comprises a group of people ... linked in a common purpose. Teams are especially appropriate for conducting tasks that are high in complexity and have many interdependent subtasks.

This is certainly true of UAT, in which a complex web of interrelated activities has to be managed effectively and efficiently to reduce the resource costs and elapsed time of the UAT exercise.

KEY ROLES IN A UAT TEAM

Business analysts (in-house or outsourced)

In any implementation project there is a potential for miscommunication between the project and the business because of differing goals and responsibilities and because each speaks its own language. Business analysts are the specialists who can speak the two 'languages' of the implementation project ('IT' and 'business') and are able to translate between them. Business analysts represent the ideas of one group to the other, ensuring that development meets the user expectations as closely as possible.

The business analyst's task of translation begins with the definition of the business requirements and the subsequent translation of the business requirements into a technical specification. Business analysts also assist in writing test cases and test scripts, matching them as closely as possible to the end-user experience, because they usually have experience of defining tests for the system test level. We must always be aware, however, that business analysts will already have a perspective on the system and may have been involved in earlier testing, so it is the end-users who must 'own' the tests in UAT.

One problem that is likely to arise is that novice UA testers take a relatively long time to create workable tests. One commonly used compromise is to involve the UA testers in the creation of UA test conditions and test cases but leave the creation of the test scripts to the business analysts.

Where business analysts are available they are usually involved in test execution and reporting, and they are particularly well placed to help rate the severity of incidents, to discount any duplicate incidents and to explain or resolve issues raised during testing.

UAT coordinator/manager/team leader (in-house or outsourced)

The UAT coordinator is responsible for creating a plan for UAT, possibly in conjunction with a test manager or project manager, and for organising and planning resources for testing. The UAT plan sets out the objectives for UAT and the activities, timescales and resources required in order to deliver UAT.

In preparation for testing, the UAT coordinator will ensure that the necessary data and environments are available for testing; accounts and logons are set up and some customer accounts and documents – or other data that are part of the end-user process – are added in order to replicate how the system will be used in real life.

During testing, the UAT coordinator will manage and track test incidents.

Incident management

An incident is defined as 'any event occurring that requires investigation', so any test that does not deliver the expected results would generate an incident, as would any defects found in documents.

Incident management (IM) is normally in place before UAT and is usually based on software tools designed specifically to support software testing. IM includes assigning a unique identification (ID) to each incident, describing the incident and adding a severity rating. The recorded incidents will be investigated by the development team and will form the basis for changes that need to be made to the software and the regression testing that is carried out as a result of the changes. Regression testing checks whether the change has been made correctly and whether other, previously working, parts of the software have been negatively affected by the change. Incidents, once raised, must be tracked to ensure that the correct process is followed (see RIAD below) and that incidents are properly closed after the retesting of any changes made.

RIAD is an acronym for the standard IM process of:

- reporting;
- investigation;
- action;
- disposal.

Each stage of the process must be 'signed off' by the appropriate authority. Only the UAT coordinator will normally be authorised to sign off disposal, which means to effectively close an incident, for UAT incidents.

The severity of an incident is assigned when it is first reported. The UAT coordinator does not necessarily assign the severity rating but may decide on the severity of incidents where there is disagreement between testers or between testers and the business analyst or developers.

Finally the UAT coordinator and the business analyst will be expected to recommend to what extent the software requires changes or whether business processes can be adapted instead. The UAT coordinator also tracks the coverage percentage (the percentage of all the possible scenarios that have been tested) and decides when enough testing has been done.

UA testers (in-house)

We said earlier that end-users carry out UAT. Those who will use the system ought to test it because of their unique relationship with the system that is both present and future. We have previously likened a custom-built system to a tailor-made garment; the only way to find out whether a made-to-measure garment fits is to try it on, and the only suitable people to try it on are the recipients.

At the UAT team level the testers may comprise both end-users and other subject-matter experts who have a thorough knowledge of the current system or the current processes. UA testers are likely to be in-house even when parts or most of the rest of the project, including UAT, have been outsourced.

Ideally the UA testers should get involved when the needs of the business are defined and the business requirements are formulated at the start of the project, so that they can represent the voice of the end-user throughout the rest of the project.

UA testers determine the appropriateness of test cases, paying particular attention to those processes that currently, or that will potentially, cause problems, thus ensuring that UAT is relevant and reflects the real user experience as much as possible. UA testers should also provide ideas on how to improve current processes or on how to change current processes if needed.

Finally UA testers will execute test scripts, note incidents that arise from those test scripts and provide feedback on the user experience.

Skills, knowledge and experience

The UAT team needs to be able to operate independently (albeit with some support from other specialists) so that it is free to manage its own operations, set its own testing standards, and plan its own schedule of tests. Independence is vital in ensuring that UAT is not driven by particular individual stakeholder interests, either in content or schedule.

The list below identifies in brackets the role most likely to bring particular skills, knowledge or experience to the team:

- in-depth knowledge of the business requirements (business analyst);
- system architecture knowledge, including current fixes and workarounds (business analyst);
- thorough knowledge of UAT (team leader);
- an understanding of formal testing methodology (team leader);
- writing a UAT plan, assigning resources and deciding which issues to escalate (team leader);
- IT literate (testers);
- considered by the user community as an expert and able to represent the wider user group (testers);
- detail-oriented and diligent in collecting proper documentation to support the test results (testers);
- creative enough to think of alternative ways of carrying out processes that may represent an improvement or may suit the new IS better (testers);
- able to feed back to their peer group in a positive way (testers).

There are other skills that may sometimes be required, depending on the size and complexity of the UAT project and the organisation's overall approach. These may include:

- knowledge and experience of test automation;
- familiarity with particular tools for requirements management, version control, IM and test planning;
- familiarity with general software tools, for example spreadsheets;
- experience of working in an agile environment.

In addition to these skills, knowledge and experience a team needs a mix of personalities that will enable the team to function effectively.

CREATING A SUCCESSFUL TEAM

Acquiring the necessary skills, knowledge and experience is a key part of creating a UAT team; the other key part is forming an effective team.

Particular tasks we have identified are normally assigned to key roles, but who delivers what on a team may differ depending on the project and the resources available. In addition to identifying the tasks and required skills for each role we need to also consider what makes any collection of individuals a balanced and successful team.

PERSONALITY VERSUS SKILL

Creating the right team is about getting the right people on the team and keeping them focused on the right things. But who are the right people?

What makes a great team is combining some qualities that are skills-based with others that are non-skills-based to make up the balance of the qualities required to get the job done. This is often overlooked when putting together a team and managers may focus too much on finding all-rounders when what they need to be most successful are flawed specialists.

The effect that personality can have on a team is also often ignored. Posing the question, 'I don't care how good he is, I don't want him on my team because...?' should help to clarify a number of non-skills-related traits that will not be helpful to creating a successful team. Attitude can enhance or diminish the usefulness of a team member regardless of their skill level.

No team is likely to be effective if it does not have the experience, knowledge or skill to carry out the required tasks.

A UAT team is not necessarily or normally a homogeneous group, each with the same set of skills, and there are other restrictions that may complicate the selection of the right set of people with the right skills. For example:

1. There is a small pool of potential candidates to choose from or the ability to reassign potential candidates' daily duties is limited.

2. Multiple roles need to be taken on by a single individual.

3. An end-user earmarked to be part of the team may leave or move jobs.

4. A specialist contractor may have the right skills but not the right attitude.

5. A potential candidate may resist taking part in UAT if they view it as an increase to their workload for no or little benefit.

Putting together a list of likely candidates is seldom as simple as ticking off the list of skills and experience relevant to each role. Furthermore skill alone does not guarantee success and it is important to consider what makes teams successful and why.

There are many approaches to making sure a team works well together to achieve a purpose. It may not be appropriate to find out what personality types the potential team members are and whether they complement each other, simply because there is unlikely to be a large enough pool of people to choose from and because there are other factors that are more important when deciding who to select (particularly skills, experience or relevant business knowledge). Nevertheless it may be helpful to consider some of the key differences in personality suggested by the kind of analysis championed by experts such as Belbin (www.belbin.com) and Myers Briggs (www.myersbriggs.org).

Whether or not you select team members based on personal characteristics, there are some general points to keep in mind when putting together a team.

Belonging to a team results in feeling part of something bigger than yourself. Each member contributes to the overall success of UAT through collaboration with fellow members of the team to produce specific results, and the bigger picture drives everyone's actions. This sense of teamwork is a team characteristic that is quite distinct from the team's ability to carry out the necessary tasks to achieve its goal. Building a successful team requires as many as possible of the following six actions in order to ensure the team has the best chance of success:

- **Communicate the purpose clearly.** Team members should understand why the team was created (its goals), its importance, where it fits into the objectives of the business and the project as well as how the work will benefit the business.

- **Ensure participants want to take part.** Members should be committed to accomplishing the objectives of the team and perceive their contribution as valuable.

- **Encourage open communication.** Successful teams are able to discuss issues in an open and friendly atmosphere and team members are encouraged to give feedback whether positive or negative.

- **Make sure the right people are present.** The knowledge and skills required to make decisions and enter into discussion must be present in order to achieve the team's goals. In an effective team all members can bring diverse opinions to the table and any conflicts are raised and addressed effectively.

- **Encourage creativity.** Delivering a new IS is partly a change management exercise and it is useful to have people in the team who are creative thinkers. It is also important for the team to understand that it can facilitate change. Involving those affected by change in decisions is a change management strategy that, all things being equal, has been shown to be effective.

81

- **Make most decisions when there is agreement.** Involving all parties in the decisions that are made may require some active intervention by the UAT coordinator if not everyone who disagrees voices their opinion. It helps to not accept the majority's opinion as a reason to make a decision but to commit to understanding all objections and dealing with those objections as much as possible.

Even where people may object to being subjected to detailed personality analysis, there are still some easily identified characteristics that can be combined within a team to great benefit and that will make the six actions outlined above more likely to happen.

SOME USEFUL 'TYPES' (FROM BELBIN)

Belbin identifies nine 'team roles' that make up an ideal team. Here are three of those 'roles' that might be usefully deployed in a UAT team:

- Monitor evaluator – characterised as sober, strategic and discerning; sees all options and judges accurately.
- Teamworker – cooperative, perceptive and diplomatic. Listens and averts friction.
- Completer finisher – painstaking, conscientious, anxious. Searches out errors. Polishes and perfects.

Others, such as team leader and specialist, have an obvious role within UAT but the emphasis here is on achieving a harmonious and effective balance between individuals with quite different characteristics.

TRAINING THE TEAM

There are three related but separate aspects to training within the project life cycle: UAT training, end-user training and planning. End-user training and planning will be explained in more detail in chapter 10:

- End-user training allows all the intended users of the system to be sufficiently able to carry out their jobs using the new IS.
- The training, planning, coordination and preparation ensure that all the required ingredients appear at the right time for successful training to take place.

UAT training provides the skills that allow the team to carry out the UAT and help to build a successful UAT team. It is hard to overestimate the importance of UAT training. UAT training is in some cases the first time the UAT team will experience the new system and often the first time it meets the project team and stakeholders. A suitable test basis has been created and the test scripts have been written. The groundwork has been laid for UAT to begin and all that remains is to execute the tests. All this preparation has cost time and money and the next step will deliver the benefits in the form of a rational decision about acceptance and a clear path to implementation.

Given this scenario, and that to be really effective UAT must be carried out by end-users, it is vital to ensure that the testing is not carried out by unprepared, untrained end-users. If participants are either not trained or insufficiently trained, there is a risk that UAT will be chaotic and unfocused and that, as a result, UAT will be unsuccessful in enabling a rational decision or collecting feedback about the status of the system and its readiness for deployment. In other words the UAT may fail to do what it was intended to do and the investment in UAT will be wasted.

LONDON AMBULANCE SERVICE (LAS) – INADEQUATE TRAINING AND LACK OF TEAM FORMATION

Before 1992, office staff were charged with deciding what ambulances should be dispatched where and it seemed that there were efficiencies that could be achieved by using a computerised system. A new computerised dispatch system was duly built and tested. Just a few hours after it was deployed problems began to arise with the new system. In the chaos that ensued during the nine days following the initial deployment 46 people died who may have been saved had an ambulance been able to get to them in time. The South West Thames Regional Health Authority report into the failures of the project identified a number of issues. In its opening paragraph it states that:

> What is clear from the Inquiry Team's investigations is that neither the Computer Aided Dispatch (CAD) system itself, nor its users, were ready for full implementation on 26 October 1992. The CAD software was not complete, not properly tuned, and not fully tested. The resilience of the hardware under a full load had not been tested. The fall back option to the second file server had certainly not been tested. There were outstanding problems with data transmission to and from the mobile data terminals. There was some scepticism over the accuracy record of the Automatic Vehicle Location System (AVLS). Staff, both within Central Ambulance Control (CAC) and ambulance crews, had no confidence in the system and were not all fully trained. (South West Thames Regional Health Authority Communications Directorate, 1993)

Taking into consideration that training was clearly not the only contributor to the far-reaching difficulties experienced by LAS, a number of lessons can be learned from the LAS case. In relation to the trial of the CAD system one of the issues reported was, 'frequent incomplete status reporting by ambulance crews caused by inadequate training, communication failures and alleged wilful misuse'.

Despite these problems having been known, the report shows that the final user training was:

- too far in advance of the implementation date leading to significant 'skills decay';
- not comprehensive and often inconsistent, problems exacerbated by constant changes being made to the system.

CAC staff and ambulance staff, roles heavily dependent on one another and often ignorant of the other's work processes and pressures, were training separately. Training the roles together would have enabled them to understand that the successful operation of the system could only come about through CAC and the crews operating in full partnership.

Training, whether related to UAT or to the ability of the user to employ the system successfully pre- or post-implementation, should keep in mind:

- Timing of the training: is it close enough to the time when the skills wll be needed? Ideally the participant of the training should move from training to use without delay.

- Does the training teach the skills that are required in order for a single user to be successful and does it teach all the skills in order for the system implementation to be successful?

- Who is trained together, does an opportunity exist to learn from other users or roles and is training an opportunity to create a team spirit?

- Is the system stable enough to conduct training?

A UAT training session should be scheduled as close to the UAT as possible and the training session should achieve three goals:

1. Introduce the project, UAT and the system.
2. Teach the skills needed for testing.
3. Discuss what being a part of the UAT team means, the benefits and the rules.

UAT TRAINING CONTENT

The content most often forgotten in UAT training is an introduction to UAT and to software testing. Unless the whole audience consists of experienced UA testers, this part of the UAT training should not be omitted or neglected. Just as incomplete requirements are created because of the author's assumed knowledge (the stuff everyone knows), so incomplete training can be created because of the trainer's assumed knowledge. A UAT training audience may have no knowledge of UAT, and may not even know what the acronym UAT stands for.

When training is delivered to groups with different levels of knowledge, as long as the introduction does not take too long, no one will complain if the training material starts at the beginning and explains the basic concepts first. In fact many people may be grateful for explanations they have always wanted to ask for but were afraid or embarrassed to. Basics to cover would include:

- General project information and timeline. (Project manager)

- The basic functionality of the system. (Project manager)

- Any known issues and workarounds. (Project manager)
- What is the system designed to deliver? (Sponsor)
- What are the expected business benefits? (Manager)
- What is UAT? (Trainer)
- What is the specific purpose of UAT? (Trainer)
- What testing has already taken place? (Project team)
- What tasks are carried out during UAT and in what order? (Trainer)

The UAT training provides a good opportunity for the trainer to discover each participant's strengths and weaknesses and for participants to recognise what their key training needs are. The interaction required to create the session, especially if members of the project team and other stakeholders deliver some of the material about the project, is invaluable in helping to form the 'UAT community'.

An introduction to the system, with demonstrations as necessary, is important so that the team can feel comfortable with the way the system works and, if possible, have an opportunity to do some simple practical exercises to gain confidence.

Task-based training

All UA testers will need to understand the key steps in executing a test script, evaluating and logging the results, and reporting test incidents. All of these will need some practical hands-on training based on the specific approach to be used in the project.

To complete the trainees' understanding of their tasks some background will be needed on the overall processes so that they can understand where their specific contribution fits. They will also need to understand the basics of how test scripts arise so that they can contribute their experience and question any aspect that does not make sense to the end-users.

The task-based training will need some background such as:

- what will happen to issues raised;
- how to feed back issues not part of the script such as usability;
- the importance of working independently and not forming a consensus.

By covering the points mentioned, the UA testers will have a good understanding of why and how they are taking part in UAT and what the outcomes will achieve.

Team formation

The single most important prerequisite to team formation is to ensure that the whole team is present. The UAT team leader will have an opportunity to assess the strengths and weaknesses of participants and begin to form a positive relationship with team members. Exercises should provide opportunities for team members to cooperate and provide mutual help and support. Group practical exercises are one way to engage team members, though it is important to watch out for the least experienced or confident being marginalised by more confident team members.

Careful debriefing of exercises provides opportunities to draw out key issues about participation and mutual support by inviting participants to make their own assessments of how successful the exercise was and how each participant contributed.

THE TEAM LIFE CYCLE

The training event is an early opportunity for the team to meet and begin to get to know each other. Even if they already know each other it may be the first time they have worked together in a team.

Every team member has three compartments to their life within a team: the tasks they must perform; their responsibilities to each other and the team; their responsibilities to themselves. In a harmonious team these three aspects are kept roughly in balance. When any one of them takes up significantly more of an individual's time and energy, the team will become unbalanced and performance will suffer. The effect of increasing work pressures as tough deadlines approach is a good example and attention to the team's health and the well-being of individuals is needed to maintain a balance.

FORMING, STORMING, NORMING, PERFORMING

When putting together a team it may be useful to remember that you cannot expect a new team to perform exceptionally from the very outset. Team formation takes time and usually follows four stages, moving from strangers or colleagues to becoming a united team with a common goal. Understanding these stages will help the manager or coordinator help the team become productive in the shortest time.

Psychologist Bruce Tuckman (1965) first came up with the memorable phrase 'forming, storming, norming, and performing' in an article for the *Psychological Bulletin*. He used it to describe the path to high performance that most effective teams follow.

Forming – stage 1

Forming is the initial stage in which members are positive and polite. Some members may be anxious because they have not worked out exactly what being a member of the team will involve. Others are simply excited about the task ahead. This stage is usually fairly short, and may only last for the initial meeting at which people are introduced to one another. At this stage the team has a high dependence on the leader for guidance and direction. The leader must be prepared to answer lots of questions about the team's purpose, objectives and external relationships and be aware that some team members may feel frustrated and anxious to get on with the tasks ahead.

Storming – stage 2

Storming soon follows and decisions do not come easily within the group. While the ways of working start to be defined you must be aware that some team members may feel overwhelmed by how much there is to do, or uncomfortable with the approach being used. Some may react by questioning how worthwhile the goal of the team is and by resisting taking on tasks. Team members may also vie for position as they attempt to establish themselves in relation to other team members and the leader, who might receive challenges from team members. Clarity of purpose increases but plenty of uncertainties persist. The team needs to be focused on its goals to avoid becoming distracted by relationships and emotional issues. Compromises may be required to enable progress.

Norming – stage 3

Gradually the team moves into a 'norming' stage as the way of working and the hierarchy is established. Agreement and consensus form among the team, which responds well to facilitation by the leader. Roles and responsibilities are clear and accepted. Big decisions are made by group agreement. Smaller decisions may be delegated to individuals or small teams within the group. Commitment and unity is strong. The team may socialise together and team members are able to ask one another for help or constructive criticism. There is general respect for the leader and some of the leadership is shared more by the team.

There is often a prolonged overlap between storming and norming behaviour: as new tasks come up the team may lapse back into typical storming stage behaviour, but this eventually dies out.

Performing – stage 4

When the team reaches the 'performing' stage, work leads to progress towards the shared vision of the team goal supported by the structures and processes that have been set up. Individual team members may join or leave the team without affecting its performance. The team has a shared vision and is able to stand on its own feet with no interference or participation from the leader. There is a focus on overachieving goals and the team makes most of the decisions against criteria agreed with the leader. The team has a high degree of autonomy. Disagreements occur but now they are resolved within the team positively and necessary changes to processes and structure are made by the team. The team is able to work towards achieving the goal and also to attend to relationship, style and process issues along the way. Team members look after each other. The team requires delegated tasks and projects from the leader. The team does not need to be instructed or assisted. Team members might ask for assistance from the leader with personal and interpersonal development.

If you are a team leader, your aim must be to help your team reach and sustain high performance as soon as possible. To do this you need to change your approach at each stage. The steps below will help to ensure you are doing the right thing at the right time:

1. Identify which stage of team development your team is at from the descriptions above.
2. Consider what needs to be done to move towards the performing stage, and what you can do to help the team do that effectively.

3.   Schedule regular reviews of where your team is and adjust your behaviour and leadership approach to suit the stage your team has reached.

If you are a team member, bear in mind the four stages and try to identify where the team is and where you are in relation to the rest of the team so that you can help to accelerate the progress towards a performing team.

DEALING WITH TEAM CONFLICT

When a number of people, each with different experiences, points of views and objectives, come together to work towards a goal, there is a chance that conflict will occur. Conflict can create an unpleasant working environment and represents a risk because the team is less likely to achieve its goals while the conflict persists.

Signs that conflict is an issue include:

- delays and absences;
- blaming and complaining;
- hostility and passive–aggressive behaviours;
- non-compliance with requests.

These behaviours alone do not necessarily mean that conflict is an issue. Deadlines may be missed and blaming may occur without conflict necessarily being the cause. If the goal of the project is understood clearly and the tone has been set for open communication within the team, you will have the best chance of avoiding conflict, but conflict can still arise because of, among other things, personality conflict, lack of skill or boredom.

The fact that conflict has occurred is also not necessarily a negative thing. Conflict that has been resolved successfully can have a positive impact on the team beyond restoring the peace. A stronger, more cohesive and productive team is likely to emerge and it can lead to personal and professional growth of the individual members of the team.

The best person to help resolve conflict is the team leader or someone who has the authority to lead in the eyes of both the business and the members of the team. This person should also be able to remain calm, factual and focused on finding a solution. The best way to resolve conflict is to establish what the issue is that is causing the problem and the most powerful way to do so is to get the team to define the issue together. Once the issue has been defined, understand the issue based on data gathered, not emotion, before deciding on the possible solutions. Managers should also examine whether they themselves were remiss when examining the causes and possible solutions of the conflict.

Some tips to help the manager or other role appointed to resolve the issues are:

- **Listen more, talk less.** Understanding where the parties are coming from is the key to finding the right solution. Encourage the rest of the team to also listen more instead of defending an existing position and to use questioning as a tool.

- **Separate people from problems.** In most cases people are not just being difficult. Finding the real and valid points of view that lie behind conflicting positions and discussing those differences means a greater understanding of issues will be achieved without damaging working relationships.

- **Focus on relationships.** As far as possible, make sure that everyone treats each other calmly and that you are building mutual respect. Lead the way by being courteous to everyone and remaining constructive even under pressure.

- **Explain the facts.** Agree and establish the objective observable facts, not emotions, that will have an impact on the decision.

- **Explore solutions.** Be open to the idea that a different solution may exist and that you can get to this idea together.

Implementing the solutions will benefit from team involvement where appropriate. If a single individual or issue has been the cause of the problems, the manager may need to take action without involvement from the team, but the actions taken to support the individual to perform better should still be noted and appreciated by the whole team.

THE WORKING ENVIRONMENT AND WORKING PATTERNS

The working environment for a UAT team can be problematic. The ideal image of a team in its own testing laboratory is seldom reality for UAT teams. A more common reality is a distributed team with members working from their own normal place of work and communicating electronically.

Environment matters to our sense of 'team' and to our sense of the importance of the task we are performing. Working in your familiar environment brings many distractions because all your day-to-day colleagues will expect you to respond to them as you would normally. The inevitable outcome of this situation is that you will struggle to get your UAT tasks completed as other priorities intrude. This is a recipe for wasted time and effort and probably a very patchy and incomplete UAT.

What can be done to achieve an ideal environment? We can split this into two components: how we achieve a sense of 'team' and how we achieve focus and commitment to UAT tasks.

For a team to perform, it must be allowed to progress through its natural growth and development and that requires dedicated time together to act as a team. It matters little what a team does in this phase as long as what it does is not seen as a waste of time and effort by team members. Training is one team activity that promotes 'teaminess'. If the team is trained as a team and the training is directed at achieving high levels of interaction and preferably some opportunities to express ideas, and discuss and agree or disagree about relevant topics, the impact on the team can be dramatic. Carefully planned preparation for UAT that includes some tricky issues to be debated (such as what do we do if pressure of work from our 'home' department affects individual performance) can have the effect of airing issues that would have to be confronted eventually anyway. Here they can be debated in a 'safe' atmosphere and team members can begin to build trust and confidence in their teammates. Keep in mind the importance of spending some of the training time on team building and spend some time before the training to ensure the trainer understands what is needed and has planned appropriate sessions (preferably spread among more conventional 'technical' sessions).

Focusing on the UAT tasks in hand is an integral part of achieving effective team behaviour. Once the team has been formed and trained, it needs to spend time together so that everyone gets a sense of the importance and priority of tasks and understands what their teammates will be doing and how they depend on our own progress to enable them to achieve their objectives. Wherever the team is expected to work from, it must find a place that is its own (even if that is a pub or café outside the workplace) so that members can spend some time together on a daily basis. This may entail 'overtime' if the only time available to meet is after work, but it might be possible to arrange a short meeting just before or after the lunch period or, better still, at the start of each day. The advantage of this is that the team meeting is an opportunity to become energised and focused on the team's needs so that team members return to their workplace in a positive frame of mind. Communication during the day, even if it is not essential to getting the tasks done, will then provide regular refreshment of the team's sense of belonging.

One good solution that takes account of the business's need to keep UAT team members engaged in other work might be to share time; half the day on routine work and half on UAT work. It is vital to align every team member's 'UAT time' and for them to have a place to work on UAT away from the normal work environment. If these can be achieved the team will have a solid base to work from.

Finally, never forget the social aspect of work and teams. If the working patterns do involve working, say, afternoons on UAT, there may be an option to extend the working day to get more time on UAT and occasionally to extend the day into an evening social event where team members can relax together and enjoy each other's company away from the pressures of work.

If you are fortunate enough to be able to work exclusively on UAT during the project, the earlier points still apply. The best time to work will probably be when the rest of the business is not around (especially if you do not have a dedicated work area) so a shift from day to evening working can be a good option.

BASIC DISCIPLINES

All that has been said about building teams and operating effectively depends on individuals behaving in an appropriate way. The team-building activities will help to resolve any dissension about behaviours but it is also good to have some rules that help the team to function. Here are some that have worked well in the past:

1. Start each working 'day' (whatever your working period is as a team) with a short (10 minutes) 'stand up' meeting in which you briefly share any problems from the previous day and any concerns about the day ahead. A 'stand up' meeting is just what it says – everyone stands because it is a short meeting and we do not need or want to get comfortable.

2.   Give your teammates respect by never being late for a meeting, review or any joint activity. That will also save the massive cost in wasted time of people waiting for others to arrive.

3.   Always get done what you have committed to. If you are absolutely prevented (by illness or by another priority forced on you) make a point of contacting your teammates to explain and apologise. It will enable them to find a way around the problem that is created for them.

4.   Keep everyone informed about anything that forces a change of plan or a delay by email or telephone.

5.   Make a point of speaking to all of your teammates at least once a day even if your work tasks do not necessitate it.

6.   Remember you will all be under pressure at some time or other. Be prepared to listen to a stressed colleague to help them to relieve the pressure they feel and be prepared to share your own stress with teammates. It helps everyone and enhances the sense of 'team'.

All this amounts to the idea of putting the team first. If every team member behaves in a way that puts the team first, they are also putting their teammates first and the impact of those simple courtesies can be significant in terms of productivity as well as making life more pleasant for everyone.

CHAPTER SUMMARY

This chapter has addressed two key concerns about teams:

- How do we select and prepare them for the technical tasks they must do as a UAT team?

- How do we build and maintain a 'performing' team?

In addressing these concerns we have also identified many of the challenges, frustrations and problems that UAT teams will have to face in doing their work effectively.

One key message that this chapter embodies is that it is never too early to begin the work of a UAT team. There is work to be done right at the beginning of the project in helping to ensure that business requirements are well defined, and there is definitely plenty of planning and preparation for the UAT exercise to be done later in the project.

Whenever and however the team is formed, there is an opportunity for UAT team leaders to begin preparing and planning how to achieve the objectives of UAT before the team is formed so that this 'shaping' work can be used to encourage team building before the team has to deliver testing under pressure.

The way the team is set up and trained will have a huge influence on its effectiveness in the face of the many distractions, frustrations and problems it will face in performing its work.

What have you learned?

Test your knowledge of Chapter 4 by answering the following questions. The correct answers can be found in Appendix B.

1. Which of the following is a key role in a UAT team?

    A. Business analyst

    B. Project manager

    C. Test manager

    D. Trainer

2. Which of the following is the second stage in Tuckman's model of team behaviour?

    A. Storming

    B. Norming

    C. Performing

    D. Forming

3. Which **two** of the following are positive actions to promote 'teaminess'?

    A. Provide everyone with a written job description

    B. Communicate the purpose clearly

    C. Encourage those with technical skills to take the lead

    D. Encourage open communication

    E. Make firm decisions and ensure everyone knows what you have decided

Some questions to consider (our responses are in Appendix B)

1. Your most knowledgeable UA tester has been identified as a complainer. What would you do?

2. One team member is being regularly distracted by their line manager to do routine tasks. How would you deal with this situation?

3. Your company does not have space to house the UAT team away from the rest of the business but is willing to give the team half of each day to work on UAT. How would you organise the team to work?

4. Your company provides a room for the UAT team to work in but takes the view that all your normal work must be completed as usual during UAT. How would you ensure that the UAT meets its deadlines?

5   UAT AS TRANSITION

In this central chapter of the book we stand back from the detail of preparation and, before we immerse ourselves in the detail of our step-by-step approach, take a look at the bigger picture. Where does UAT fit in the larger scheme of things? What are its core functions and attributes? What overall contribution does it make?

Topics covered in this chapter

- The IS life cycle as a series of transitions
- Planning for transitions
- UAT as a transitional phase
- UAT as an event and UAT as a process

THE IS LIFE CYCLE AS A SERIES OF TRANSITIONS

In the introduction we presented the idea of the IS life cycle and here we reproduce the life-cycle model we included there as Figure 5.1.

The model reminds us that UAT is not just the end of development; it is the beginning of the period of service use. The life-cycle image provides a clear sense of how things change over time and where the effort and cost go, and these are important to bear in mind.

But UAT also acts as a gatekeeper for another key transition: it marks the change of ownership of the ideas embodied in the software from the development team back to the users. Remember there was another of these tricky transitions earlier on, between requirements and development. Actually the transition was from the users' understanding of what they needed to the developers', using an RS as the translation document and the symbol of exchange.

So another way to look at a life cycle is as a series of transitions from one state to another via transactions. Generation of the RS was the first transaction; UAT will be the second. There are more significant transitions ahead. Once the system is implemented and initial teething problems are sorted out, the system will transfer into routine maintenance and this will entail a transaction between the development team and the maintenance team.

Figure 5.1 The IS life cycle

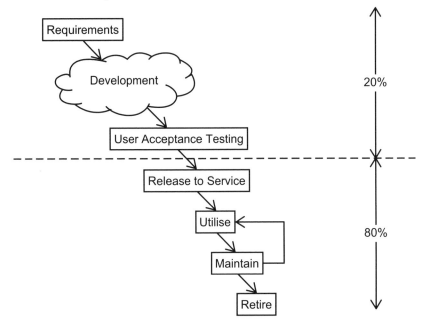

There will then be a period of enhancement and improvement while the sponsor seeks to get the maximum value from the IS with the help of the user community. Once this has been achieved a further transition occurs to transfer ownership from the sponsor to the business to manage any further enhancement together with the maintenance team. Notice that each of these transitions involves a transaction between two groups: users to developers to create the RS; developers to stakeholders at UAT; developers to maintainers when maintenance begins; sponsor to the business when routine business use begins. Figure 5.2 illustrates these transitions.

Figure 5.2 A map of transitions

Users	Dev Team	Dev Team	UAT Team	UAT Team	Sponsor	Sponsor	Business
Requirements Elicitation	Development		Roll-out		Shake Down		Service Use
	RS		UAT		System Release		Handover to the Business

The point of all this is that these transitions are the points in the project when change occurs, where value is released and where problems can occur. They are the critical points in the overall life of the IS.

The reason we are particularly interested in transitions is their capacity to cause problems. That is one reason why we prepare very carefully for them. We have explained how much effort goes into the transition from ideas into a RS (and how rarely the transition goes smoothly even then), and in Chapter 4 we touched on the significance of training as a means of preparing for the UAT transition. We will rely on training again to ease the transition into service use.

Figure 5.3 Preparation for transitions

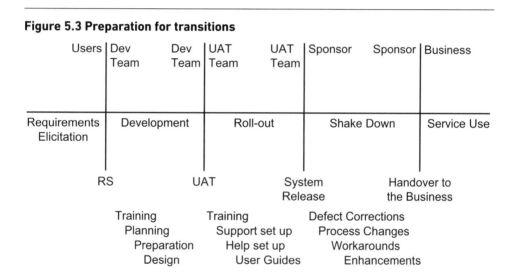

PLANNING FOR TRANSITIONS

UAT is the key transition that we will focus attention on, but it is worth noting briefly that the series of transitions we have identified all need careful preparation. Two activities need to be happening continuously throughout the life cycle to enable and encourage the difficult changes in perception that end-users, in particular, will have to face: these are communication and training.

This is not the right place for a detailed discussion of either of these activities, except to say that their significance justifies detailed planning to ensure that the right activities occur at the right stage. Appendix C provides a slightly more detailed look at how training can be managed as a perception-changing process throughout a project in relation to UAT. A communications plan structured similarly would also be a valuable tool for keeping all parties not only informed but prepared for the next step.

UAT AS A TRANSITIONAL PHASE

The ultimate goal of UAT is that the current status of the system is understood and either we know the system is ready to be deployed or we understand what needs to happen for the system to be ready for deployment. An unsuccessful UAT will mean that the deployment of the system is placed in jeopardy.

UAT is the key transition point between ownership of the project by the development team and ownership of the system by the business because it sets up the whole phase of in-service use (potentially 10–20 years) during which the system will deliver value.

Figure 5.4 illustrates UAT as a transition phase. As we showed in Figure 5.3, transitions need preparation because they entail changes of perception and process – changes that humans find difficult and stressful – so we need to build up to them over a period. The preparation for UAT is a vital part of achieving effective UAT and this in turn impacts directly on the quality of the accepted system. We want to be able to verify not just the quality of the system but how well it serves its user population, how well it enables business objectives to be achieved and how well it will cope with changes and updates in future.

Remember that this 'in-service use' of the life cycle accounts for around 80 per cent of the total life-cycle cost and the extent of that cost will depend on two parameters:

- the quality of the system as accepted (because this is the base for all future changes and development);
- the buy-in of the end-user community (because this, more than anything else, will impact on how much business benefit is eventually achieved).

We know that end-user buy-in is important to the success of the IS yet end-user buy-in is a difficult thing to define and to achieve. We need to achieve the willingness of the user community to accept ownership of the system (warts and all) and a commitment to work with it to achieve what the business needs from it. Without this buy-in every minor defect can be a 'show-stopper' and future change can be very difficult to achieve.

UAT AS AN EVENT AND UAT AS A PROCESS

In order to enable the UAT transition to be smooth and effective, the preparation needs to be started early. End-users who have never tested a system before need to be trained – and training in this case covers not only unfamiliar territory for them but also requires them to think differently about the systems they use. The changes of perception this requires cannot be achieved in a one-off training course just before UAT begins; they will take gentle introduction, reinforcement and gradual extension over a period so that the change of perception is not just superficial. As we will see in the next few chapters, end-users will also have tasks to do to prepare for the UAT 'event' including planning, analysis and design, as well as familiarisation with the system, the business processes and perhaps some tools so that the test execution and reporting stage can be completed effectively and efficiently.

Figure 5.4 UAT as transition

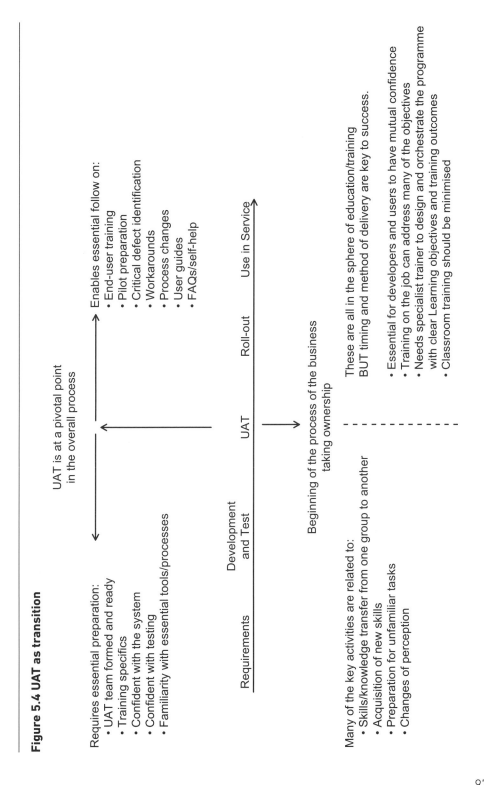

UAT is at a pivotal point in the overall process

Requires essential preparation:
- UAT team formed and ready
- Training specifics
- Confident with the system
- Confident with testing
- Familiarity with essential tools/processes

Enables essential follow on:
- End-user training
- Pilot preparation
- Critical defect identification
- Workarounds
- Process changes
- User guides
- FAQs/self-help

Requirements   Development and Test   UAT   Roll-out   Use in Service

Beginning of the process of the business taking ownership

Many of the key activities are related to:
- Skills/knowledge transfer from one group to another
- Acquisition of new skills
- Preparation for unfamiliar tasks
- Changes of perception

These are all in the sphere of education/training
BUT timing and method of delivery are key to success.

- Essential for developers and users to have mutual confidence
- Training on the job can address many of the objectives
- Needs specialist trainer to design and orchestrate the programme with clear Learning objectives and training outcomes
- Classroom training should be minimised

The UAT 'event' is actually a process that begins very early in the life cycle, and many of the key decisions and preparatory actions need to occur well before the 'event' if UAT is to be successful.

As we step through the stages of the UAT process it will be important to bear in mind the timing of the actions we describe and of the training that might be needed to enable them. There are many views on when the UAT process should begin, but the process we will describe is at least as important as the development process and should, in our view, begin at the same time. It will progress at a slower pace and consume much less resource, but it is a process that, like training, should be running in parallel with development from beginning to end.

CHAPTER SUMMARY

This chapter has taken an overall view of UAT as a transitional phase and as a continuous process requiring early preparation. After reading this chapter you should be able to answer the following questions:

- How can IS development be viewed as a series of transitions?
- What is the role of UAT as a key transition?
- What transactions are needed between groups at the UAT transition?
- When should the UAT process begin?

Some questions to consider (our responses are in Appendix B)

The project you are working on is acquiring a COTS-based suite of applications configured to meet your company's needs, but there are some known potential gaps in functionality. Implementation is scheduled for 12 months ahead and a UAT team will be formed 1 month before UAT.

a. As UAT team leader elect you have been asked to review the plans. What feedback would you give?
b. As a nominated end-user tester for the UAT team, what would you propose?

6 PREPARING FOR UAT – PLANNING

We need to begin our UAT exercise as we begin any important exercise – by deciding what it is we are trying to achieve. By the time we get to UAT you may think this should be already well defined but remember that change is the curse of planning. There will have been many diversions from the original plan and requirements – both accidental and deliberate. Right here and now is where we must finally decide what we believe the project's business objectives are – the business intent – and what the system to meet those objectives must look like.

The way we shape, plan and prepare for UAT will determine how effective it is. In this chapter we address all the key elements of planning for UAT. Those key elements can then be packaged into a UAT test plan. We have not covered the generic elements of routine test planning, which can be found in almost any testing textbook and which are well covered by standards such as IEEE 828, preferring to focus attention on those things that are unique and important to UAT.

Topics covered in this chapter

- Deciding what we want to achieve
- Acceptance criteria
- UAT objectives
- Entry criteria
- Defining the testing we will need
- Creating a test basis for UAT
- Setting up the test management controls

THE UK PASSPORT AGENCY – THE IMPORTANCE OF PLANNING

In the summer of 1999 the UK Passport Agency brought in a new Siemens computer system without sufficiently testing it or sufficiently training staff on how to use it. At the same time an unusually high demand for passports was driven by a change in the law, which meant that children under the age of 16 required their own passport when travelling abroad. The combination of the two factors resulted in a backlog of 565,000 passport applications and the Home Office was forced to pay out millions in compensation for missed holidays and staff overtime.

The National Audit Office report into the passport delays found there to be three main causes:

- a lack of adequate planning and testing of the likely time needed for staff to learn the new processes;
- insufficient contingency planning, which led the pilot test phase to be extended before the issues it raised had been fully overcome;
- a lack of communication with the general public.

Despite the fact that the pilot implementation showed that the new system produced lower volumes of passports than expected, it was decided to roll out the system to the rest of the passport office locations. As part of the pilot the old system had been removed and the new system was installed. The decision to implement, or as the UK Passport Office described it 'extend the pilot', was made because the old system was deemed outdated and potentially not year-2000 compliant, and returning to the old system was deemed costly and risky. What was not known at the time was that the expected demand for passports had been greatly underestimated and that when the demand for passports grew, bringing in extra staff and overtime would not have the expected positive impact on productivity because the extra human resources could not overcome some of the limitations of the system.

One of the key recommendations issued from the National Audit Office was:

Project managers should plan for adequate testing of the new system before committing to live operation, in particular for staff to learn and work the system.

The difficulties experienced at the UK Passport Agency are relevant to the effort of planning in a number of ways. The example illustrates the importance of:

- the complexity of implementations and the outside influences that affect what decisions are made regarding the extent of testing required or when to cease testing;
- understanding the difference between testing and implementation;
- understanding the acceptance criteria and the potential risks that arise when acceptance criteria are changed.

DECIDING WHAT WE WANT TO ACHIEVE

Before we commit resources to doing any testing we need to be sure we are testing the right things in the right way. We have some deliverables from the development project as a starting point:

- a set of business requirements in the form of an RS that most likely will have changed;

- some testing done by the development team and perhaps also by some independent testers that may or may not be well documented;

- a system that should be complete and ready for UAT;

- a trained UAT team ready to begin its work.

This is our starting point, but what is our end point? How will we know that we have finished UAT? Our next step is to decide these things so that we can use them to identify how good our starting point is and to plan a way to get to our desired end point.

ACCEPTANCE CRITERIA

We have to have a way to decide when to stop testing and release the system into operation. The decision is not ours to make, but the decision maker(s) will need some good objective information to help when making a judgement and it will be our job to provide as much of that information as we can.

Acceptance criteria are measures of what the sponsor and users want that we can use as a target to aim for at the conclusion of UAT, but they also act as a basis for gathering and reporting information.

The obvious acceptance criteria might be that the system works correctly, has no defects and is ready for release on the planned release date. There is certainly nothing wrong with those criteria – but what if they cannot all be achieved? If some of the criteria are unachievable in a reasonable time frame, how do we decide what to do? This is the reason why release decisions can become more emotional than rational – the objectivity provided by setting criteria for acceptance is compromised if any one of those criteria is found to be too difficult to achieve for one reason or another and the rational discussion that generated the criteria in the first place needs to be repeated when the participants are under the stress of delivery deadlines.

The statistics from The Standish Group and others suggest that there is quite a high likelihood that we will not achieve all three of the 'obvious' criteria together. We will have to make decisions about what to do when we are under pressure from users and from the business to get the system into service as fast as possible, and that is why we need to set realistic acceptance criteria well before UAT begins. By realistic we mean recognising the likelihood of not achieving an ideal outcome and planning to limit how far we allow ourselves to deviate from the ideal. If criteria are based on the worst scenario we can accept, they become realistic because everyone involved in the decision knows that failing to achieve them is not just letting go of the ideal but opening up the real possibility of failure.

How do we identify realistic criteria? We start from the 'ideal' criteria:

1. The system works correctly.
2. The system has no defects.
3. The system is ready on launch date.

Now imagine that we are at launch date, UAT is not yet completed and there are 20 defects outstanding. What should we do? It all depends...of course. There are two extremes. At one end the time pressure is so great that the other criteria have to be ignored, so we release and deal with the problems as they arise. At the other we are under no time pressure so we complete UAT and fix all the defects before we release. Neither of those extremes is likely to be the reality so we need to decide how much room for manoeuvre we have in each of the three key criteria.

If we take the time criterion, we need to understand how critical the release date is. What will happen if the system is not released on that date? What costs will be incurred? How will business be affected? How much delay could be tolerated? How quickly would the costs and problems ramp up with a delayed release date?

For the defects criterion we need to decide on criticality. Some defects are more serious than others. We could split defects into three types: critical, serious and routine:

- A critical defect is one that will prevent the system from delivering its core capabilities or achieving its business benefits.

- A serious defect is one that is not critical but will impair performance significantly. There may be ways to offset the problems – 'workarounds'.

- A routine defect is one that can be fixed routinely because it does not significantly impact on the performance of the system.

We can obviously not tolerate any critical defects, but we may be able to tolerate some serious defects and many routine defects. Bear in mind that the numbers are important. Releasing with 10 routine defects should not have much impact on the system; hundreds of routine defects, on the other hand, may have some impact and may also take some time to correct. So the scale goes from zero defects of any kind at one end, to zero critical defects, 'a few' serious defects and unlimited routine defects at the other end. Of course three levels of criticality can be expanded to five, seven or however many you need.

The functionality criterion is simpler. There is obviously some functionality (and some non-functional behaviour) that is critical to the system and, by the same token, there is some that is almost cosmetic in nature. It is common to consider three levels of criticality for system functionality:

- Essential functions are those without which the system cannot achieve its business benefits.

- Important functions are those that are not critical but the system will not perform as expected without them (there may be ways of working around the missing functions, though there might be some training or retraining needs as a result).

- Cosmetic functions are definitely not essential but they may enhance usability or save time or effort.

One simple way to deal with this criterion is to prioritise functions for testing so that the essential functions are tested first, but we may still have a less than ideal scenario when planned testing time is exhausted.

Now there are three interacting criteria to consider and any decision impacts all three. If, for example, we decide to fix all the critical defects pre-release, it will have an impact on testing because the fixes will need to be tested.

There is no simple formula that provides the ideal set of release criteria, nor is there a guaranteed outcome from any choice that we make at release time. The point here is that it is essential to think about acceptance criteria well before they are used so that everyone understands the relative importance of each criterion, data can be collected and tracked to ensure that performance against each of the criteria can be accurately reported, and rational decisions can be made when they are needed.

UAT OBJECTIVES

The other side of acceptance criteria is the strategy they generate. Acceptance criteria that make system functionality paramount will encourage a strategy that puts progress with testing ahead of defect corrections, with the possible impact of delays while critical defects are fixed. Acceptance criteria that make the delivery deadline paramount will encourage prioritisation and early defect fixing to minimise the likelihood of delay, but possibly at the expense of completeness of the system at release. The acceptance criteria alone provide a goal but they do not define a strategy.

Acceptance criteria define the status of the system at release but they are not helpful in deciding how to achieve that status. We need to consider how best to manage UAT to achieve the acceptance criteria: we need a UAT strategy. As well as achieving a goal, a strategy needs objectives that define the way the goal is approached. In the case of UAT we have to consider the reasons we do UAT – to reduce risk, to gain confidence, to assess the readiness of the system for live use and to facilitate the transition to live use. Each of these is an objective that we could track, for example by checking off risks against a risk register or by measuring readiness against a checklist.

As with acceptance criteria we need a mix of objectives that enable us to approach the acceptance criteria in a way that does not neglect any aspect of UAT but ensures that attention is paid to each aspect by measuring progress towards it during the testing. All four of the primary objectives will be likely to feature in a UAT strategy and generate key milestones that enable the team to track progress towards the acceptance criteria.

ENTRY CRITERIA

Recall now our deliverables from development:

- a set of business requirements in the form of an RS that most likely will have changed;
- some testing done by the development team and perhaps also by some independent testers that may or may not be well documented;
- a system that should be complete and ready for UAT;
- a trained UAT team ready to begin its work.

Are these all in place and in a state that we can work with? Are the project and the system ready for UAT?

By way of example, imagine what would happen if we began UAT with 20 critical defects outstanding – the system code would be changing frequently and in critical areas so every test we did would be invalidated by a change within days and we would have to repeat it. This would be an expensive waste of time, but worse still, it would make change control so complex we would be at risk of losing control of the state of the system code or the testing.

To avoid this kind of problem we need some entry criteria for UAT to give UAT a reasonably 'clean' start. Like acceptance criteria these will typically be based on outstanding defects, any outstanding testing and any issues raised by the development team and not yet resolved (such as the inability to complete system testing because no test environment was available).

Like acceptance criteria, entry criteria can be simple. Here is a possible set of criteria:

- All testing up to system testing is completed.
- No defects are outstanding.
- No issues are unresolved.

These are all eminently sensible criteria. However, we need to be a little more pragmatic and flexible to avoid logjams. So perhaps more realistic criteria might be:

- All testing up to system testing is completed with no outstanding incidents.
- No critical defects.
- Not more than five serious defects.
- Not more than ten routine defects.
- No issues affecting testing are unresolved.

Even these might be negotiable, but they do set a target for the development team to achieve for a handover to UAT. Equally important they give the UAT team some leverage. If a project has had problems and is running late, there could be a lot of pressure to just get UAT done so we can get the system into service. The pressure is understandable, but what value would UAT add under these circumstances? None at all. It would simply be a case of completing an activity because it is on the project plan.

At this critical stage in any project it is vital that decisions take into account all their implications for the project, for the system, for the users and for the business. Entry criteria have no absolute power and cannot prevent bad decisions, but they do at least make the nature of the decisions visible and they enable the risks associated with a decision to be assessed.

Once we have achieved the entry criteria we are ready to begin the testing, or at least the planning.

DEFINING THE TESTING WE WILL NEED

Our work on acceptance criteria and UAT objectives has provided us with targets. The acceptance criteria tell us what the business needs are and the UAT objectives tell us what UAT needs to achieve.

Now we can use our testing skills to decide how we will achieve the objectives in a practical and effective way. We define a UAT strategy to identify what needs to be tested and to what level, and from the strategy we can build a plan that we can execute.

At this stage much depends on the size and complexity of a project. In some cases a set of UAT objectives, a strategy and a plan might seem like overkill. If a project is genuinely small and simple it may be feasible to define some acceptance criteria and to use these directly for defining the tests, missing out all the intermediate steps. These are decisions that can only be taken at project level. If you have understood the purpose of a UAT strategy and plans then you will be in a good position to decide what level of detail is needed in these stages or even whether they are needed at all. Be careful, though, that your judgement is a rational one and not based on time, management or any other external pressure. It is always nice to be popular, especially with superiors, but popularity can be very short-lived if the outcome is bad for the business.

Defining a UAT strategy

A UAT strategy is our way of combining acceptance criteria and UAT objectives, all based on stakeholder priorities and concerns, to arrive at a set of milestones and a set of measures by which we can determine progress at each step. From there we can begin to define the testing activities we will need to achieve each of the milestones.

As testers we will have our own view on what the testing priorities should be. Should we test the most important functions first or the most frequently used? Should we test that the most serious risks have been averted or start with the easy low-risk areas to build up some early confidence?

Defining a strategy is about confronting all the choices and making a decision on priorities that gives us a path that delivers value.

Figure 6.1 is a very rough schematic but shows how cost and value relate to each other in an IS project. The development phase is all cost. In an ideal delivery – on time, on budget and UAT successful – the system then begins to add value, first recovering the cost of development and then yielding net benefits to the business over time. In a late and over-budget delivery, but one where testing and UAT are deployed effectively to ensure the best outcome, the total cost is higher and the delivery of net benefits is delayed, but the eventual success of the system is still assured. In the third case, where a late and over-budget development is forced into an on-time delivery by reducing the time and cost of UAT, the value-add line is flatter as a result of problems not resolved before delivery that plague the system's effectiveness, slow down the ramp-up of benefits, delay the recovery of costs and the point where net benefits are achieved and reduce the eventual benefits to the business.

Figure 6.1 The cost and value of a system

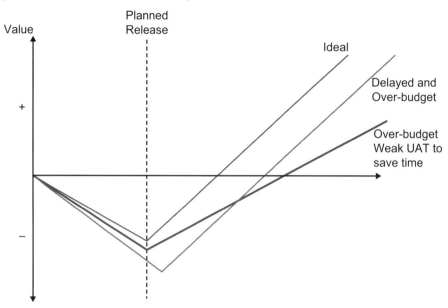

Of course this is just a schematic and has no specific values assigned. It merely identifies the nature of the risks. The final curve may not be as flat as it is drawn – but equally it may be flatter. One effect not shown in the schematic is the impact of release before issues have been resolved. The impact of this could be a further delay and cost as critical issues are addressed to enable users to begin building value with the system.

The purpose of the schematic is to invite the very important discussion about the implications of release decisions. The outcome of the discussion will be a strategy that achieves an acceptable line on the diagram, and that will incorporate an appropriate UAT strategy.

High-level test planning

Once a UAT strategy is settled the high-level plan can be created to define how to test to the required level, meaning what tests are required and how they should be organised for an effective and efficient UAT.

Identifying test environments

Tests will typically need a test environment that is as close as possible to the live environment. For each test we need to identify what test environment will be needed and how it needs to be set up to support the tests.

CREATING A TEST BASIS FOR UAT

We have three useful methods for discovering what updates or extensions may be needed to the RS: reviews, structured interviews and observation.

Reviewing existing requirements

Chapter 2 explained the reasons why the RS is almost certainly no longer up to date or complete by the time the UAT preparations begin. Even if it was possible for the business representatives to define perfectly what they need from the IS at the start of a project, mistakes will creep in as more people interpret the requirements based on their own assumptions and as the needs of the business change over time. Changes may also have been made to the system that were not updated in the RS.

We need to review the original requirements, together with any changes that have been made to the RS, to determine whether they accurately represent what is being delivered and whether they now reflect user expectations.

Review team

The review team needs to include the author of the original requirements if they are still available, the individual(s) who will be designing the tests for UAT and the UAT leader. In fact it would be beneficial for the all UAT team members to be involved in the requirements review because they will gain familiarity with the requirements and the rationale behind the system that has been built as well as being able to bring their user perspective to bear on the review to identify any changes or additions that would make the UAT specification more practical and realistic as a test basis.

Preparation

Strictly speaking no preparation is needed for a walk-through, but there is a lot of value in reading and absorbing the content of the RS and this is an exercise that will have to be done at some stage to enable testing to proceed smoothly. Better to do it now as preparation for testing than later, because the preparation can be turned to immediate and good value.

The preparation is simply to read the document, taking careful note of any aspects that appear to be incomplete or incorrect, noting any questions you have and preparing your own notes as an aide-memoire for the review meeting so that you do not forget important points in the heat of the moment. A checklist may help the reviewers, especially those new to UAT, focus on the types of issues they will need to look out for, such as:

- **Problems:** anything that the reviewer thinks would not work in real life.
- **Inaccuracies:** anything that the reviewer thinks is a mistake or misinterpretation of the requirement.
- **Ambiguities:** any requirements that can be interpreted in more than one way or cannot easily be tested.
- **Omissions:** anything the reviewer feels is missing from existing requirements, any requirements that are missing from the document and any other omissions such as the lack of unique IDs.

- **Clarity:** spelling, grammar and quality of written text are not important in themselves but they are very important if they tend to confuse the reader or make reading the document difficult.

A checklist can also be used to convey the important message that the exercise is focused on error detection, not correction. This means that the reviewer does not need to know what the requirement ought to be, only know or suspect that it is incorrect.

The aim of the review is to identify important deficiencies in the RS that may have led to errors in implementations (to help target testing) and to identify gaps that make it likely the implemented system will not meet the true business requirements.

Conduct

The walk-through should be conducted in a relaxed and informal way but with some control over the time. Normally the author would lead a walk-through, but for UAT it might be advantageous to ask the UAT leader to chair the meeting. Reviewers should be encouraged to raise questions and make comments freely and a scribe should be appointed to capture all comments that lead to any actions (such as updating the specification). Discussion can be free as long as time is not being wasted. It is important to adopt the right tone so that the author in particular does not feel threatened – always remember you are commenting on a document and not on its author. The comments should be impersonal and objective, with no suggestion of criticism or blame.

The chair may have to step in from time to time to ensure the meeting progresses and does not get bogged down in detail – a useful rule being that the review should identify issues but not try to resolve them. In practice the simplest ones can probably be resolved there and then, but discussion needs to be limited if a quick resolution is not found – the issue can then be documented for follow-up later.

Reviews that last more than a couple of hours tend to become quite tiring and less effective as time goes on. If it is clearly impossible to complete the requirements review in two hours, a second review meeting will need to be convened to complete it.

Follow-up

Follow-up for a requirements review will have two components:

1. The author completing any actions or changes agreed and documented at the meeting. These will be primarily to enable test planning and test design.
2. The UAT leader taking note of any areas of the requirements where there are concerns about completeness and correctness so that testing can be targeted on these.

The review chair should take responsibility for checking with the author that any changes are done within a reasonable time frame, bearing in mind that design of the tests for UAT cannot progress until any significant changes have been made to the requirements documentation.

When requirements are being reviewed as a prelude to UAT, the important defects in the document are those that will affect testing.

Exercise 6.1

Case study: requirements review
One of the Excelsior plug-ins allows users to request approval for absences via the system. Table 6.1 shows some of the requirements that this absence request and approval functionality were built on. Using the criteria for the walk-through checklist and the information provided in Chapter 2 about what makes a good requirement, note down any issues you can find with the requirements as if you were part of a review.

Table 6.1 Absence requirements

Reference	Category	Description	Priority
A4.0	Absence request	Users should be able to see a calendar containing colleagues' approved absences prior to booking their own absence	2
A4.1	Absence request	The number of remaining days off for the holiday year should be visible throughout the absence request process	1
A4.2	Absence request	Remaining days off should be recalculated when they are booked as absence on the calendar according to Absence Rules 2012 specified in this document	2
A4.3	Absence request	Users should be able to change absence days in the calendar	2
A4.4	Absence request	No absence days should be carried over to the new holiday year	2
A4.5	Absence admin	Admin users should be able to add and subtract days, overriding the standard calculation described above	1
A4.6	Absence admin	All changes by admin users should be tracked and be auditable	3
A4.7	Absence approval	Managers should only be able to approve absence for the members of their team and not their own absence or those of users senior to them	1
A4.8	Absence admin	A system reminder should notify users of any remaining days off that will soon expire	3

Our answer is in Appendix B.

Interviewing stakeholders

The best way to find out what user expectations are is to ask the users! The problem we may run into is that expectations may have moved on a long way since the requirements were first written, and not necessarily in a realistic or practical way in every case, so we have to do some careful sifting.

Other stakeholders, especially the sponsor, can act as a balance so we need to carry out a fairly systematic review of stakeholder expectations across all the main groups – sponsor, users, managers and developers. We need to include developers to ensure that if we capture expectations that were not originally requirements, they are actually feasible and achievable in a realistic time frame. So this is a tweaking exercise, not an opportunity to rewrite the requirements. Having said that, the opportunity to air their views can be a significant driver towards getting users' support for a roll-out, even if not all their expectations are met.

The vehicle for gathering expectations is a semi-structured interview. The structured part will ensure that everyone is asked the same set of questions to give us a consistent set of information. The unstructured part is about giving individuals the opportunity to expand on their answers and express their concerns and wishes in a more complete way.

Observing user processes

If we are not already familiar with the way users work in the organisation, or if the new system will involve significant changes to the way users work, or if the system is the first IS in the organisation, we need to understand what is currently happening so that a smooth transition can be made to the new system. The transition is not in itself part of UAT, but UAT must ensure that the system is capable of handling the way users are expecting to work.

Capturing user processes is a delicate area because much depends on how prepared the organisation is for the change. By the time UAT is being planned, users should already be aware of what will happen after the system is operational. Training should have at least begun and processes should have been mapped out. If all this has happened the transition may be well in hand and we will have access to the information we need to build tests that follow the new user processes.

In the event that transition is not as well advanced as it should be, however, we need some basis for constructing tests that can enable users to interact with the system in a realistic way. If we observe how users work now we can at least make a reasonable assessment of how the user processes will need to change to work with the new system. Observations can then be recorded in a form that facilitates test design – the ideal recording method is to construct user stories and use cases, which we turn to next.

Building use cases and user stories

User stories

As we explained in Chapter 2, user stories are not really requirements but they are a good way to capture and document some of the key user expectations. For UAT we will need to spend time with as many users of any existing system and any designated users of the new or updated system as we have time for. Capturing their views in user stories will be a relatively quick and consistent way to create a consolidated picture to supplement the RS.

We described what user stories look like in Chapter 2, but here is a quick reminder.

CAPTURING USER STORIES

User stories are used mainly with agile methods as a means of gathering requirements, but they can be valuable as a means of expressing requirements or to summarise requirements information whenever tests are being designed.

A user story is made up of one or two sentences in the everyday language of the end-user that covers what a user needs to do as part of their job function.

Example:

- As a team member I want to be able to complete a contract so that it can be processed.

- As a manager I want to be able to approve a contract created by my team.

The user story normally takes the form: 'As a <role> I want <goal or desire> so that <benefit>', although the benefit may not be stated where it is implicit. The alternative syntax is 'In order to <benefit> as a <role> I want to <goal or desire>.'

Example 6.1 – Excelsior requirements update
The business requirements for Excelsior were captured at the start of the project in an RS. However, at least one key requirement was omitted and, since the requirements were written, circumstances have changed, which has resulted in a number of the requirements being out of date:

1. New company rules state that all employees must have their expenses approved and this no longer, as was previously the case, excludes managers.

2. No requirements exist to allow executive assistants (EAs) to manage requests on behalf of managers in any part of the system. If this functionality were not provided, EAs would have to log on with the manager's logon details, causing a potential audit and HR issue.

3. No requirement was captured to identify an invoice as 'third-party billing', which the organisation needs to capture for reporting purposes and for managing disbursements – expenses incurred as a result of client work by a third party that may be treated differently by the taxman.

The development team is aware of the first two new requirements and the code has been written to deliver them, but the changes were not captured in the RS. The UAT team has carried out semi-structured interviews to try to capture all the current user requirements and collated and analysed the data. A meeting has been organised to create user stories based on the interview findings. These are the resulting user stories:

- **1.1.** As a manager I want to be able to send my expenses for approval.
- **2.1.** As a manager I want to be able to assign my account to my EA so that they can manage the request process on my behalf.
- **2.2.** As a manager I want to be able to approve a claim managed by my EA.
- **2.3.** As an EA I want to be able to assign my account to another EA in my absence.
- **3.1.** As an account manager I want to be able to mark an invoice as third-party billing.
- **3.2.** As the accounts director I want to be able to unmark a contract as third-party billing.

Use cases

Use cases are often used to capture current processes and can bridge a gap between requirements written by users in plain language and the more technical specification language. As we explained in Chapter 2, a use case describes the interactions between a role (actor) and a system in order to achieve a particular outcome, using diagrams or simple structured text. The actor can be a person or another system that our system will interact with.

We will return to the Excelsior case study in a moment. First let's further examine how use cases are written using the relatively straightforward example of an ATM.

Example 6.2
If the system we are implementing is an ATM, the use cases should identify the high-level processes that the user needs to be able to carry out. So in the first instance we may identify that there are two things the user needs to be able to do; withdraw cash and order a statement. The initial use cases can be listed in a use case grid that provides the basis for the use case exercise.

Table 6.2 ATM use cases

Use case no.	Use case name	Primary actor	Priority
1.	Withdraw cash	Customer	1
2.	Order statement	Customer	1

There is no one right way of writing a use case but a style that is commonly used is:

- Title
- Actor(s)
- Main success scenario
  - Step
- Extensions
  - Extension

Here is a primary use case for withdrawing cash.

Title: Withdraw cash

Actor(s): Bank customer (any bank), banking system

Main success scenario: Any bank customer can obtain cash from their bank account

Basic path:

1. The customer puts a bank card into the ATM.
2. The ATM verifies the card's validity.
3. The ATM checks the country of issue.
4. The ATM requests a PIN.
5. The customer enters their PIN.
6. The ATM validates that the PIN is valid for the bank card.
7. The ATM presents options including withdraw cash.
8. The customer chooses withdraw cash.
9. The ATM presents options for amounts of cash.
10. The customer chooses an amount or enters an amount.
11. The ATM checks that it has enough cash in the ATM.
12. The ATM checks that the customer is below withdrawal limits.
13. The ATM checks that there are enough funds in the customer's bank account.
14. The ATM debits the customer's bank account.
15. The ATM offers the option to print a receipt.
16. The customer selects the print receipt option.
17. The ATM returns the bank card.
18. The customer removes the bank card.
19. The ATM prints the receipt.
20. The ATM issues the cash.
21. The customer takes the cash.

The steps represent the path through the system to allow cash withdrawal and states how each of the actors interacts with the system. This use case is also known as the 'sunny day' use case or primary use case, because it is the path that is most likely to occur when all goes well. In order to complete the creation of the use cases, 'rainy day' scenarios or edge cases must also be written. These represent the alternative paths if something goes wrong, for example what the path should be if the customer does not have sufficient funds in their bank account in order to withdraw the amount requested.

One common way to note the alternative paths is to enter the alternative steps below the primary use case. The whole process does not need to be described in full, only the steps that are different for each alternative path.

It is easier, more efficient and good practice in terms of risk management to write the sunny day scenarios first and derive the edge cases from them. If lack of time becomes an issue, the most important use cases will have been written first.

Edge cases from the ATM use case would have to cover how to deal with:

- an invalid bank card;
- a foreign bank card;
- an invalid PIN entry;
- an invalid amount entered;
- insufficient cash in the ATM;
- customer going over withdrawal limit;
- insufficient funds in account;
- insufficient paper in the ATM to print a receipt;
- customer not taking the cash.

There will also be edge cases that may happen but are less likely to, for instance how the system would deal with the inability to debit the account. The goal is not to define every possible use or edge case but to find the common use cases and prioritise accordingly. The use cases and edge cases can be circulated round the UAT team to get feedback on whether the most likely important scenarios have been covered. It is then up to the business to decide how much time and money should be spent testing the scenarios that are less likely to occur.

Creating the working requirements set

From our reviews, interviews and observations we should now have a reasonably complete picture of what the system needs to do to meet expectations. If we record all this information, as far as possible, in the form of user stories and use cases we will have a good basis for building tests. If the original requirements are not in this form we can make a judgement, depending on how much has changed and how complete the requirements were originally, about whether to convert all our information to a common format.

Exercise 6.2

Can you think of three other user stories that could be added to those listed above that relate to a manager sending expenses for approval, a manager assigning an account or third-party billing contracts?

Our answer is in Appendix B.

Example 6.3 – Excelsior case study

At a high level the user stories we generated in Example 6.1 defined what is missing from the current Excelsior requirements. After further discussion it was decided that user story 2.3 was not required and that it would be more efficient to change the business processes instead. It was agreed that managers would deal with any requests themselves (functionality captured in the original requirements) or that direct reports would be notified of the EA's absence.

The user stories, apart from user story 2.3, were signed off by the stakeholders as the requirements that need to be added to or changed in the RS and that need to be tested during UAT. Other less important issues that were discovered were deemed insignificant and ignored or added to the list of change requests to be included in future releases. The project team then set out to create use cases based on the user stories.

Table 6.3 Expenses use cases

Use case number	1.1
Application	Excelsior – Expenses
Use case name	Approve manager expenses
Use case description	A manager has expenses they wish to be refunded for; they will enter the expenses claim, attach images of the receipts, and send it for approval with the intent of getting the expense claim approved and paid
Primary actor	Manager claiming expenses
Precondition	Manager must be logged on to Excelsior and have claim-able expenses
Basic flow	1. The manager selects Expenses module from the main menu
	2. The system verifies the role
	3. The system applies the role limits to the expenses page
	4. The manager enters each expense item in the relevant category section
	5. The manager adds the VAT amount
	6. The manager adds images of the receipts
	7. The manager saves the expenses sheet
	8. The system checks that all the required fields have been completed
	9. The system checks that a receipt has been added for each item
	10. The system checks the claim is below the expenses limit
	11. The manager selects the send for approval option

12. Excelsior Expenses sends a notification to the manager's approver

Alternate flows
4a. The manager enters an expense item into the wrong category

4b. The system displays an error message 'Incorrect category'

5a. The manager adds the wrong VAT amount for the VAT category

5b. The system displays an error message 'The VAT category or VAT amount is incorrect'

8a. The manager has failed to complete a required field

8b. The system marks all required fields that have not been completed in red

8c. The manager completes the required fields – back to 7

9a. The manager has not added a receipt to one of the expense entries

9b. The system displays an error message 'Expenses items without receipt may not be reimbursed' 'Return' 'Continue'

9c1. The manager selects the return option

9c2. The manager adds the missing receipt(s) – back to 7

9d1. The manager selects the continue option – back to 10

10a. The manager's expenses claim is above the expenses limit

10b. The system displays an error message 'Your expenses claim is above the approval limit by £x' 'Return'

10c. The manager selects return and reduces the expense claim by the amount on the error message or more – back to 7

Use case number	**2.1**
Application	Excelsior – Admin
Use case name	Assign an account to an EA
Use case description	A manager would like an assistant to check and manage expenses claims from their direct reports
Primary actor	Manager assigning the account
Precondition	Manager must be logged on to Excelsior

Basic flow	1. The manager selects Admin module from the main menu
	2. The manager selects the 'Assign my account' option
	3. The system displays the assign to options
	4. The manager enters the name of the user to assign to
	5. The manager selects the apply option
	6. The system checks that the assistant has an active account
	7. The system assigns the assistant to the manager's account
Alternate flows	6a. The assistant does not have an active account
	6b. The system displays an error message 'Inactive account' – back to 4

Use case number	**2.2**
Application	Excelsior – All self-service modules
Use case name	Manager approval of assigned request
Use case description	A manager has assigned their Excelsior account but wishes to approve the requests
Primary actor	Assistant
Precondition	Assistant must be logged onto Excelsior and be in receipt of a request that requires approval
Basic flow	1. The assistant opens the notification from Excelsior for approval of a self-service request
	2. The assistant checks the request details
	3. The assistant marks the request as complete
	4. The system presents notification options 'Email' 'System' 'SMS'
	5. The assistant selects an option
	6. The system sends the details of the request to the manager with options 'Approve' 'Decline'
	7. The manager selects the approve option
	8. The manager selects the apply option
	9. The system notifies the manager of the outcome of the request
	10. The system notifies the assistant of the outcome of the request
	11. The system notifies the requester of the outcome of the request

Alternate flows	2a. The request is incomplete
	2b. The assistant marks the request as incomplete
	2c. The system returns the request to the requester – back to 1
	5a. The option selected has not been set up for the manager
	5b. The system displays an error message 'Option is not available' – back to 5
	7a. The manager selects the decline option
	7b. The manager enters a decline reason – back to 8

Use case number	**3.1**
Application	Excelsior – Contracts
Use case name	Add third-party billing
Use case description	An account manager is creating a contract and wishes to mark it third-party billing in order for the VAT to be applied correctly to disbursements
Primary actor	Account manager
Precondition	Account manager must be logged on to Excelsior Billing Contract creation and a contract must be selected
Basic flow	1. The account manager selects the contract type
	2. The system offers the contract type options
	3. The account manager selects the third-party billing option
	4. The system marks the third-party billing check box on the contract
	5. The system applies third-party VAT information to the contract
Alternate flows	None

Use case number	**3.2**
Application	Excelsior – Contracts
Use case name	Add or remove third-party billing
Use case description	An account director checks contracts and wishes to correct contracts marked third-party billing incorrectly in order for the VAT to be applied correctly to disbursements
Primary actor	Account director
Precondition	Account director must be logged on to Excelsior Billing Contract creation and a contract must be selected

Basic flow	1. The account director selects the third-party billing contract
	2. The system displays the contract
	3. The account director deselects the third-party billing option
	4. The system deselects the third-party billing check box on the contract
	5. The system removes the third-party billing VAT information from the contract
Alternate flows	None

SETTING UP THE TEST MANAGEMENT CONTROLS

While we are defining the testing we also need to bear in mind the management of defects – those already identified before UAT starts and those we find as we do our testing. These defects will affect the acceptance decision so effective tracking and accurate counting is crucial. Test logging will also be a key discipline so that we can tell at any time how much of the planned testing has been completed and how much is still left to do. Finally we will need to ensure that change control is in place to ensure that all changes to the system or the tests are identified and followed up. Every defect will potentially lead to change in the system code and the tests, and every update to system code will generate new tests to check the defect has been corrected and also regression tests to ensure nothing else has changed. We need this not only to ensure we are always testing the latest version of the system code after changes have been made but also to identify the 'tail' of testing that follows each change so that we know what additional testing is required over and above what was originally planned.

Change control

The change control mechanism will already be in place because the developers will have used it throughout development. You may need a briefing on how to access it and interpret the information, and that will be a good initial point of contact with the development team if you are not already working together. The development team can then show you the state of the system code at the point of handover so you can see for yourself what changes have been made and what testing might be outstanding from any recent changes.

You will need to bring your test cases and test scripts under change control in case they later need to be changed and also so that the links between system code and the tests run on it are clear; the maintenance team will need this later.

Test logging

Test logging ensures that we know which tests have been run and which have not; therefore it also helps us to estimate what testing still needs to be done and when it should be complete. The test logs may give us some information that we can use to streamline testing or to add new tests to the plan. We need to set up a test logging mechanism before we start testing.

A test log is really a simple list of tests that have been designed and scheduled so that you can identify when each is complete. In practice we need a little more information because we need to capture any changes made to tests, any rescheduling of tests for whatever reason, and any follow-up to test failures, such as the retest and any regression testing being entered into the log.

The log will capture every test completion and its outcome so we can easily generate valuable statistical data from it to measure progress against objectives and to predict our completion date on a dynamic basis. We will need to create a test log before we begin test implementation. There is an example of a test log in Chapter 8 that you can use as a starting point. Implemented as a spreadsheet it provides a simple tool to use and from which to gather data.

Incident reporting and defect management

Incidents are the outcome of any test failure. We call them incidents because we do not know yet that we have found a defect; we only know that the actual result of the test does not match the expected result. This could be due to a defect in the system but it could also be a defect in the test or in the test environment, or the tester may have simply made a mistake. The incident report should enable a developer to repeat the test and get the same result so that they can diagnose the cause.

IM becomes defect management when an incident is diagnosed as a defect in the system code or documentation. Other outcomes will need to be followed up by changing tests or some other action. As for test logging, IM systems are usually based on databases so that data can be collected, analysed and reported – we will need this to determine whether objectives have been met.

Like change control, IM should be in place and the development team can brief you on how to raise incidents and define reports for your own use. If the IM system is automated, it will incorporate a workflow element so that the steps required to clear an incident will be managed by the tool; if not, there will be a process defined that you will need to become familiar with.

CHAPTER SUMMARY

In this chapter we have covered the very important first step of planning our UAT exercise. As with all complex activities, UAT needs to be meticulously planned so that we know exactly what we need to do, when, how and with whom. Equally importantly we need to communicate to everyone what is going to happen so that they can make their contribution. Finally the plan needs to identify what we will do when things go wrong so that we can deal with the situation effectively and efficiently without introducing delays or uncertainty.

After reading this chapter you should be able to answer the following questions:

- How do I make sure I have the right requirements as a test basis?
- How do I decide what testing I need to do?

- How will I know when I have done enough testing?
- How will I know if the results are acceptable?
- What will I do if things go wrong?

What have you learned?

Test your knowledge of Chapter 6 by answering the following questions. The correct answers can be found in Appendix B.

1. Which of the following is a valid UAT objective?

   A. To ensure the system is delivered with no defects
   B. To remove all risks from the system before release
   C. To ensure the risk of releasing the system is acceptable
   D. To complete everything in the UAT plan

2. Which **two** of the following would be valid as acceptance criteria for a system?

   A. All planned testing has been completed
   B. There are no outstanding change requests
   C. There are no outstanding test incidents
   D. There are no serious defects
   E. All essential functions have been tested

3. Which of the following must be addressed in UAT?

   A. Business requirements
   B. User stories
   C. Use cases
   D. Business processes
   E. User expectations
   F. Technical specifications

Some questions to consider (our responses are in Appendix B)

1. You are finding that users are reluctant to express ideas about what they expect from the system when it is delivered and fall back on what is in the requirements. What would you do?

2. The sales manager believes that acceptance criteria should not delay delivery to customers who have expectations of early delivery. The development manager believes that acceptance criteria should include only requirements coverage. The marketing manager is concerned about the image of the business and insists on zero serious defects as an acceptance criterion. What should you do?

3. The development team is reluctant to give the UAT team access to the incident reporting system because it could result in lost incident data if someone makes a mistake. What would you do?

7 TEST DESIGN FOR UAT

Chapter 3 introduced the test development process (TDP), the process by which the tests for UAT are created. Each of the three components of the TDP, test conditions, test cases and test procedure specifications (test scripts), represents a step in a process or hierarchy that starts with the definition of the requirements and ends with UAT.

In this chapter we will explore that hierarchy, explain in more detail how test conditions, test cases and test scripts are built, and apply this directly to our UAT exercise.

Topics covered in this chapter

- The hierarchy of test design
- Identifying test conditions
- Designing test cases
- Designing test scripts
- Data creation

THE HIERARCHY OF TEST DESIGN

Test design

The process of transforming general testing objectives into tangible test conditions and test cases.

The levels in the test design hierarchy (see Figure 7.1) are as follows:

- The business requirements represent the needs of the business.
- The test conditions state what aspects of a given requirement should be tested.
- The test cases specify, for each test condition, what preconditions, inputs, expected results and post-conditions apply.
- The test procedure specification lists the steps the UA testers will carry out for each test case and identifies the test data to be used for each test.

Figure 7.1 The test design hierarchy

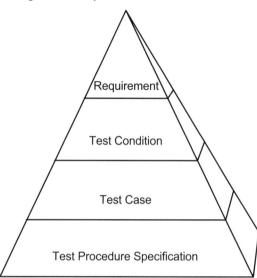

The test design process starts at the top of the hierarchy: the test conditions are identified from the test basis, test conditions are turned into test cases and the test cases are used to create the test scripts.

The relationship between the documentation levels is maintained by assigning a unique reference number to the requirements and referring all the following documentation back to the requirement from which it arose. This is known as traceability. Traceability is the key to ensuring that the test design covers all the requirements in the RS and no others. It will also become invaluable in managing documentation changes, so that when any document in the hierarchy is changed it will be easy to find out which related test conditions, test cases and test scripts must also be changed.

Test design does not deal solely with how to write individual examples of test conditions, test cases and test scripts; it also defines how to manage the process of writing all the test conditions, test cases and test scripts in a way that is efficient and effective. All of the test design phase, but particularly the creation of the test conditions and test cases, should be carried out with assistance from the end-users in the UAT team, bringing together the expertise of UAT with expertise of the business to create the best and most relevant test materials. At a minimum a representative of the business must sign off the requirements, the test conditions and test cases as complete and accurate, but this is a poor substitute for direct end-user involvement in test design. Tests defined by others will almost certainly lack the unique end-user perspective that makes UAT an effective tool in reducing risk.

IDENTIFYING TEST CONDITIONS

Test conditions are the first step in the creation of tests. Test conditions are logical statements that represent some aspect of a requirement. In other words, a single test condition is 'something that can be tested.' Each test condition represents a single component of a feature that can be assessed as either true or false and the feature is correctly implemented if and only if all conditions are true.

Depending on how business requirements are written, one requirement can give rise to many test conditions. In Chapter 3 we used a login example and noted some of the variations that ought to be tested. Each variation equals a test condition. We will use the same example and look in some more detail at the requirements for login to the system.

Example 7.1

Table 7.1 Login requirements

Reference	Category	Description	Priority
FR 4.1	Security	End-users must be able to log on to the system using a username and password	1
FR 4.1.1	Security	The username is the user's company email and is not case-sensitive	3
FR 4.1.2	Security	The password is case-sensitive	2
FR 4.1.3	Security	The password must be at least six characters long and contain at least one number	2

The test conditions must represent every variation of test that together would confirm that the requirement has been met. The three test conditions we identified in Chapter 3 were as follows:

1. If a valid username is entered with the correct password, the user is logged in to the system.
2. If a valid username is entered with an incorrect password, an error message appears.
3. If a non-valid username is entered with a password, an error message appears.

These are the relevant test conditions for requirement 4.1 but there are some more conditions we can identify based on requirements 4.1.1 to 4.1.3.

4. When a valid username is entered in all caps with the correct password, the user is logged on to the system.

5. When a valid username is entered in all lower case with the correct password, the user is logged on to the system.

6. When a valid username is entered in caps and lower case with the correct password, the user is logged on to the system.

7. When a valid username is entered with a password containing fewer than six characters, an error message appears.

8. When a valid username is entered with a password containing no numbers, an error message appears.

It is more efficient to note down all the possible test conditions that can be conceived of, even if it seems that there is an overlap between them. It is easier to combine duplicate test conditions than it is to spot ones that are missing. In any case a list of test conditions, even when based on the requirements, is not guaranteed to be an exhaustive list, but is a list of the things we can think of to test.

Getting team members or other end-users to review the test conditions should lead to useful feedback and ideas for further conditions. In our example what qualifies as an overlap depends on the error messages. If unique error messages need to appear such as: 'Passwords are at least six characters in length' or 'Passwords contain at least one number', more test conditions are needed than if the error message is generic for all login failures.

Because conditions 4, 5 and 6 all require entry of a valid username and password – one where the username is entered in caps, the second where the password is entered in lower case, and the third where the username is entered in both caps and lower case – test condition 1 is no longer required. You could also argue that test condition 6 is not required and is adequately tested by a combination of conditions 4 and 5. If, on the other hand, you tried to combine condition 4, which checks that the password entered in all caps is allowable, with condition 7, which checks that a password with fewer than six characters is not allowed, this cannot provide an answer to both conditions in one test. If we enter a password of fewer than six characters in all caps and the login succeeds, we know there is an issue and requirement 7 has not been met, but if the login fails, we cannot deduce from the test result whether the system will allow caps in the username.

Creating the test conditions is a crucial stage in the test design process. For simple functionality, such as logging on to the system, you could still logically deduce what testing might need to be done without writing the conditions down, but being able to conceive of all the possible test conditions is vital when it comes to more complex system functionality. In order to make sure that all the requirements have been covered, and covered in enough detail, it may be useful to create a matrix. Matrices are widely used in testing and help to compare the content of one document against another. For example a matrix could show the functional requirements that have been created for each business requirement.

Similarly a spreadsheet can be created that shows the requirement ID and the requirement description horizontally and each of the test conditions alongside the requirement in columns. Table 7.2 is an example of a matrix matching conditions related to the Excelsior contracts functionality to the business requirements. The requirements identify the required functionality and the conditions for the basic testing that should be carried out in order to test that the functionality worked.

Table 7.2 Test condition matrix

Spec/Design ref	Ref	Req name	Condition 1	Condition 2	Condition 3	Condition 4	Condition 5	Condition 6
1. Creating contracts	1.1	Create a Contracts Category	Create a Contracts Category on Excelsior – Contracts	Create a Contracts Category page	Add a link to a contract	Add a contract note	Check Category status is New	
	1.2	Create Contracts Sub-category	Create a Contracts Sub-category on Excelsior – Contracts	Create a Contracts Sub-category page	Link to a main Contract Category page	Check link works		
	1.3	Check main Contracts user interfaces	Create a contract workspace	Delegate a task	Go to My Contracts page	Create link to other part of Excelsior – Contracts such as FAQ	Link two contracts through collaborative partners	
	1.4	Check Contracts Supplier user interfaces	Create Contract workspace	Delegate tasks	Go to My Contracts page	Create link to other part of Excelsior – Contracts such as FAQ		

(Continued)

Table 7.2 (Continued)

Spec/ Design ref	Ref	Req name	Condition 1	Condition 2	Condition 3	Condition 4	Condition 5	Condition 6
2. Sharing contracts	2.1	Share a contract	Go to Excelsior - Contracts	Share a contract with the UA tester to your left				
	2.2	Amend a contract	Go to 'Contracts shared with us'	Share a contract with the UA tester to your left	Check contract documents can be viewed and edited	Add a contract note	Add a calendar entry	Create a task
	2.3	View amended contract	Go to Excelsior - Contracts	Go to the main Contracts page	Ensure the changes from 2.2 are visible on the main Contracts page			

This type of matrix is easy for all interested parties to understand and sign off.

Most implementations are going to yield a large number of test conditions and risk analysis may need to be carried out to determine which test conditions are most important. Entering the test condition into a spreadsheet or matrix has the added advantage that the test condition can be linked to the requirement (and the requirement's priority) and that the information needed to create the test case can be added to the same spreadsheet.

DESIGNING TEST CASES

We previously learnt that a test case specifies the preconditions, inputs, expected outputs and post-conditions for a test of whether a test condition is true:

- The preconditions and post-conditions identify the state the system must be in before the test is executed and the state it will be in after test execution, respectively. Understanding what the start and end 'state' of each test will be helps to identify the sequence the testing should be carried out in for the most efficient UAT session. If a number of test cases have the precondition that the user is logged on to the system, it would make sense to run the login tests first. That way the time involved in carrying out tasks that are not part of testing is kept to a minimum.

- The test input data state what the entries in to the system should consist of in order to test the condition. Defining the data entries for the test case is an important part of preparing the test data for UAT. In Example 7.2, unless the implementation is for a change or addition to an existing system, in which case real user accounts may be replicated, test accounts will need to be created with usernames and passwords. These accounts must support the different user roles that will be accessing the new system.

- The expected output from a test case is the vital element that enables us to determine immediately, objectively and consistently whether a test has passed or failed when it is executed.

The test case contains all the basic information required in order to test, but without the form (the test script) that the end-user will need to identify the specific data to be used at test execution time and to record the outcomes of testing.

Example 7.2

Here is a simple test case for a login procedure.

Table 7.3 Login use case

Test condition	If a valid username is entered with the correct password, the user is logged in to the system
Preconditions	User is not already logged in Test user account has been set up
Input data	Valid username Correct password
Expected result	User login is successful
Post-condition	User is logged in to the system

Practical user testing

In Chapter 3 we considered different ways of constructing tests using standard test-case design techniques and more practically oriented approaches such as requirements-based, risk-based and process-based testing. Test-case design techniques will prove very helpful in generating specific test cases to support our overall approach, but we should also use our applied common sense and experience to produce tests that work for users and provide meaningful results.

We also learned that we are testing a system, not just a piece of software, and that we are interested in what the system can or cannot do for users. We are not particularly interested in whether the software performs according to its technical specification because the developers and testers will have already tested the system from that perspective. Our concern is not about compliance with specification; we are using the RS as a basis for our test plan mainly because it gives us a well-defined scope for our operations.

Focus on what matters – test by risk

The idea of risk-based testing is useful here. If we have an understanding of what aspects of the system are most important and might cause a serious problem if they were not effective, that is if they represent risk, we can prioritise tests by risk level and test the highest risk areas first. We can begin by identifying the risk level for each requirement or group of requirements and putting them in priority order. That is at least a practical starting point for developing test cases.

Test at the edges

We have already pointed out the fact that boundaries and edges are rich with problems, so it is a good idea to focus attention on the edges. To do this you can use BVA with or without EP – they are related techniques but independent. You can exploit BVA wherever you find a boundary.

Remember also that we are not only interested in boundaries within programs. Business processes have edges and boundaries and these will also be a good place to explore.

So when you are building test cases for a business process, make sure some of them explore the edges of the process.

Keep the tests simple – test by practical scenarios

If we know how the end-user expects to use the system and what business processes will interface with it, we can set up some practical scenarios that represent commonly used processes and build test cases around them. The collection of processes will have some patterns – hierarchical, time-based, customer-based or some other pattern. The patterns can be exploited to link together similar processes so that we can test a whole area of the system at one time with a relatively small set of test cases and test data.

One further thing to consider is sequencing the tests. Remember in the definition of test cases we ran into 'execution preconditions' and 'execution post-conditions'. These are no more than the definition of the way the system needs to be set up to run a particular scenario (that is an execution precondition) and the state the system is in when the test scenario is complete (that is an execution post-condition). The advantage of identifying these pre- and post-conditions is that we can match them up: a test scenario with a precondition that matches the post-condition of another scenario can be run immediately after that scenario with no additional setting up.

There are other ways we can link test scenarios together to make the testing more meaningful and more convenient to run by saving us setting-up time. We can sequence tests by date and time so that each scenario is in a natural date and time sequence from its predecessor. If there are scenarios with no time gaps, we can run them without breaking to reset the system date and time. Similarly if one test updates a database and another test reads the database, we can again use the natural sequence to save time.

The key idea is to organise the tests by scenario and then look for patterns that can be exploited to make the testing easier and more natural.

The overall aim of UAT is to determine whether the system can be effectively used by its intended end-users and all of your tests should reflect that. What we need are simple tests – simple to implement and interpret – that directly exercise the things that users need to happen.

Concentrate on typical and unwanted scenarios

If it proves difficult to prioritise test scenarios by criticality, frequency or value, we can use our previous experience to identify what is a 'typical' scenario, meaning a scenario that will be used often and that perhaps underpins other more complex scenarios. This is testing by 'mainstream' activities. Even if they are not the most critical, they will be the most often used so problems with them will cause user frustration and potentially damage productivity.

We can similarly look for the scenarios that represent our worst nightmare – the things that should never happen. If we test these, we can gain confidence by discovering that worst cases actually do not happen or we can identify early a situation that could prove fatal for acceptance. This is an example of an extreme scenario; something at the edges or boundaries of system behaviour. The BVA test-case design technique can be useful here to test relatively few cases that are on or near this boundary – either inside it or outside it – and gain confidence that the system will not stray outside.

Exceptions are the things that do not fit the normal rules. They are similar to edge cases because they may generate a different way of processing data than that used for the bulk of the system. If there is anything wrong in these areas, it may only involve a relatively small area of the system but it will generate those mysterious errors that never seem to get sorted out.

Look for any exception cases in the RS, the business processes, the user interface or anywhere else you can think of. The effort will be well worthwhile.

Make the scenarios work together

It is a small step from the idea of end-to-end testing to the idea of linked scenarios. Building up a sequence of scenarios that represent a typical working day is one way of linking scenarios together. Not only will this make the testing realistic, it will also make it easier to implement and it will take advantage of the fact that, in many cases, the post-condition of one test will automatically match the precondition of another.

Take this a step further and use the working day at the beginning or end of a week, a month, a period or a year and we will end up testing some of the most important boundary cases for the business.

A little imagination goes a long way in inventing and linking scenarios to achieve multiple testing objectives. It saves time, adds realism, increases efficiency and, best of all, it means the UAT will be able to maximise the amount of testing it can cover in the time available.

Make use of business processes

Business processes should already be documented at this stage. They will almost certainly involve data entry and use of output data, as well as some interactive dialogue with the computer. We need to identify these flows so that we can build end-to-end tests of business processes. Within the end-to-end tests we have the opportunity to introduce specific test cases of interest so we need to construct scenarios with data that will be flowed through the system during the end-to-end tests. That way we get confidence in the processes, the system's interface with the processes and the specific data handling that is part of the processes.

Test in cycles

Testing can be time-consuming and expensive to set up because we have to test many scenarios, each with potentially different starting conditions. If we can group tests together that have a common starting point or use a common test environment, we may be able to make the tests more effective, quicker and more cost-effective to execute and easier to manage at the same time.

We can also test time-related aspects of the system by running tests in cycles. Each test cycle has a different starting point in time and in system status, so the input cycle might run first, followed by an update cycle and so on. This will enable us to generate input data for each cycle from the cycle before.

Focus on the user interface

One of the principal reasons for having users test systems before they come into use is because the users have a unique perspective on whether a user interface actually 'works'. Detailed usability tests may or may not have been done on the system but, whether they have or not, the system needs a user's evaluation.

How 'comfortable' is the screen layout? How are data entered? Are fields sensibly located for ease of data entry? How fast can you carry out your most common actions? Can you achieve the kind of throughput that has been specified for the system? Users have an internal specification for a good user interface and the system needs to be tested against it. The tests will be informal and mostly embedded in other tests, such as tests of business process flow, but it is vital that concerns about the user interface are highlighted through incident reports.

This is not the same thing as usability testing, which is more technical system testing, but users will be interacting with the system. If you have been trained on how to use the system before you begin testing, you will be able to identify any user interface problems that training does not prepare you for, and your insights into what works well and what does not should be recorded. So although we will not design usability, reliability, availability or a host of other specialist tests, we will be able to raise incident reports on any aspect of the system that causes us concern about how it will behave when newly trained users are expected to use it to deliver real results.

Think about performance

Related to the user interface evaluation, we need to know how easily and quickly we can work with the business process data requirements. This is not a formal performance test (some formal performance testing may well have been done during system testing) but it is a final check that the system can deliver the throughput needed to achieve the proposed business benefits.

Remember negative testing

We explored some negative test cases when we looked at BVA, but it is useful to be aware that UAT can often focus on those tests that are positive in nature. A positive test is one that demonstrates that something that should happen does happen – a function works, for example.

Negative testing is concerned with ensuring that what should not happen does not happen. This is a much more difficult and time-consuming approach to testing because there are many more negative test cases than positive test cases. Here is a very simple example.

Example 7.3

An input field is defined as a six-character alphabetic field. A valid input will have up to six alphabetic characters. Any other input is not valid and should trigger an error message.

As a positive test we can enter a single alphabetic character, two alphabetic characters and so on up to six alphabetic characters. The system should respond according to the input data.

Negative tests must now fill in all the other possibilities: an empty field, a field containing five alphabetic characters and a single numeric character; and a field containing one or more of the non-alphanumeric characters. A complete set of negative tests would need to include every possible combination of six keyboard characters that is not in the range of one to six alphabetic characters.

This is daunting, but is it important? It is clearly important to confirm that the system will recognise input that is not valid and behave appropriately because users will inevitably make mistakes at some point in the future and we do not want the system to respond in a way that will cause problems (for example by 'freezing' the input screen).

We cannot exhaust all possible negative tests for each and every scenario because it would take an infinite amount of time. We equally cannot ignore negative testing because the impact of an inappropriate response will be unknown. There has to be a compromise.

The most effective compromise is to add some negative testing to every positive test, using what we already know about user behaviour such as the most common keying errors. If we give some thought to the kinds of mistakes users are most likely to make and run limited negative testing around those mistakes, we can ensure we have made the system a little more robust than it otherwise would be. Negative testing is one good way to exploit the benefits of EP and BVA.

Things that we should not test

Just to reinforce what has already been said about usability testing and performance testing, we should not test what has already been tested, nor things that we are not technically competent to test, nor things that we do not have a test environment for.

Regression

If we raise incident reports that identify defects that are subsequently fixed, we need to rerun the test that originally failed. We will also need to schedule some regression testing to check that the changes made have not affected any other part of the system.

Testing perspective

When you have considered all these alternative approaches and weighed them up, always bear in mind the single most important idea behind UAT. It is the end-user perspective, the end-users' instincts for what will or will not work, the end-users' experience and the end-users' common sense that will generate the best tests for UAT. Identifying all the ways things can and do go wrong in a system they have previously used will provide a long list of relevant tests without even thinking about techniques or theory.

DESIGNING TEST SCRIPTS

Detailed or high level?

Some user tests are designed in such detail that the user merely executes the test script and reports whether the program passed or failed it. This is a good way to design tests if your goal is to provide a carefully scripted demonstration of the system, covering all the processes and inputs you need to test.

If your goal is to discover what problems a user will encounter in the real use of the system, your task is more difficult. UA tests are quite expensive to administer and the risk is that they may not yield much useful information. A good user test must allow enough room for cognitive activity by the user while providing enough structure for the user to report the results in a way that is useful to those who have to fix the problem.

The answer is to provide a mixture of high-level tests and more detailed testing in order to capture all the processes and data that need to be covered and the issues that may arise as a result of a more intuitive approach to using the system by the end-user. High-level tests can contain as little information as 'log on and book a training course', while detailed test scripts may go down to a level that elaborates all the steps defined in the test case.

Preparing a simple test script

Test scripts are the lowest-level detail required to run the test. Usually when we refer to test scripts we mean the formal documents that describe the test steps and expected outcomes in detail and allow the tester to note any errors against those detailed steps. Test scripts can also be informal and you may find that a lot of useful feedback comes from a test script that simply says: 'Log on and request a day off.' Formal testing is required for UAT so it is important to remember that the kind of feedback received from informal testing may not relate directly to whether specific requirements were met. We can easily make the informal test formal by creating a simple script.

Example 7.4

Table 7.4 Simple login test script

Login1: Normal user login

Requirement ID	FR 4.1
Purpose	Users are able to log in with an acceptable user ID and password
Precondition	User is not logged into the system. Test account has been set up successfully
Test data	User ID: tester1@acme.com Password: UAT1
Process steps	1. Click system icon 2. Enter User ID 3. Enter password 4. Click Login
Expected result	User is logged in to the system on the Home page
Post test	User tester1@acme.com is logged in
Notes	

Test scripts versus test cases

If a test case describes a single piece of functionality that requires testing, then every test case will require a test script. A script should be created for each test case because the purpose of the test script is to provide the detailed test steps to the UA tester. Essentially, for a given test plan, you should only need to run a single test script to consider that the test case has been executed. If you need to run more than one, the test case contains multiple conditions and more test cases are needed (one for each condition).

However, test scripts are more flexible than that. A test case can be run many times with different input data with a single test script, or a number of different data entries can be tested as part of the same set of test scripts to cover a number of different test cases.

Test scripts are not usually executed in isolation but combined into a collection that represents a scenario, perhaps related to a single business process or different elements of a user interface. The scenario should represent a process or actions that otherwise logically follow one another or represent different data entries that test the same field or functionality.

Example 7.5 The Excelsior Contracts system

This example relates to part of the Excelsior system called Contracts. The Contracts functionality allows users to create, manage and store contracts that the organisation has entered into, or intends to enter into, with suppliers and third parties.

There are two user roles that interact with the Contracts functionality in specific ways:

- The Contracts team member can create and manage the contracts but not approve them.
- The Contracts team manager cannot create or manage contracts but can approve them.

The Contracts system allows users to see and access contracts from a number of different views that represent the status of the contract:

- new;
- in progress;
- awaiting approval;
- approved;
- declined;
- signed;
- archived.

The test scripts below have been written to check that for each of the two user roles, the system displays the correct status, columns, data and links on the In Progress screen. The In Progress screen lists all the contracts that have not been finalised and have not yet been sent for approval.

4.11 Test script 17 – Check the functionality on the In Progress view
Purpose: ensures the In Progress view contains the expected columns and that data are mapped correctly, displaying documents with a status of In Progress appropriate to the user role.

4.11.1 Test criteria/procedure

1. Check the In Progress view contains the expected columns for a user with the role of Contracts team member. Check the document details are as expected for a user with the role of Contracts team member, the content of the data on the view are mapped to the correct columns and the links on the screen function as expected.

2. Check the In Progress view contains the expected columns for a user with the role of Contracts team manager, Check the document details are as expected for a user with the role of Contracts team manager, the content of the data on the view is mapped to the correct columns and a link to approve the document details is available to the Contracts team manager.

Test #1 – Check the In Progress view contains the expected columns for a user with the role of Contracts team member.

Test step	Test description	Expected results	Pass/Fail comments and observation numbers raised
Scenario 1 – Logged into Excelsior Contracts with the user role of Contracts team member			
This scenario tests: • The correct columns are shown in the In Progress view. • The correct links are available.			
Expected results: • The column names included are as listed below. • The links of Update Document and Reassign Document are available to the Contracts team member.			
1.	Access the In Progress view by selecting the In Progress view on the left side of the screen	In Progress view displayed	
2.	Ensure the correct column names are displayed	The following column names are expected to be displayed in the order listed from left to right: • Industry • Supplier Name • 3rd Party Name • Contract ID • Contract Name • Contract Date	

(Continued)

Test step	Test description	Expected results	Pass/Fail comments and observation numbers raised
3.	Ensure the correct links are available against each contract	The following two links are not expected to be available against each contract: • Update Contract • Reassign Contract	

Test #2 – Check the In Progress view contains the expected columns for a user with the role of Contracts team manager.

Test step	Test description	Expected results	Pass/Fail comments and observation numbers raised

Scenario 2 – Logged into Excelsior Contracts with the user role of Contracts team manager

This scenario tests:
• The columns are included in the In Progress view.
• The correct links are available.

Expected results:
• The column names included are as listed.
• The links of Update Contract and Reassign Contract are not available to the Contracts team manager.
• The link to approve contract is available.

1.	Access the In Progress view by selecting the In Progress view on the left side of the screen	In Progress view displayed	
2.	Ensure the correct column names are displayed	The following column names are expected to be displayed in the order listed from left to right: • Industry • Supplier Name • 3rd Party Name • Contract ID • Contract Name • Contract Date	

(Continued)

137

Test step	Test description	Expected results	Pass/Fail comments and observation numbers raised
3.	Ensure there are no links available against each contract to update or assign a contract	The following two links are not expected to be available against each contract: • Update Contract • Reassign Contract	
4.	Ensure a link to approve the contract is available	The following link is available: • Approve Contract	

Note that, as is the case in the example used above, information from the test procedure and the test case, such as the expected results and the preconditions, may also appear on the test procedure specification. This makes it easier to understand and schedule each test case without having to read the test steps.

DATA CREATION

Creating the master data that can be used for testing by the business users is a key part of the preparation for UAT. Before any test script is executed the correct test data must be available in the system and no test should fail because the correct data were not available to be selected or otherwise used by the test team.

What is test data?

When the test cases are created the input data are noted on the test case or a list of possible input values may be provided for UAT. All the input data that are going to be tested should therefore be a known quantity. Test data also extends to the data that need to be available in the system for testing to be completed successfully. Test data are any kind of input, any kind of file that is loaded by the application, or entries read from a database. This may require you to create logins and passwords and any data that testers must verify or use. A great starting point to determine what data you need is to look at the business processes and then look at the scripts. For example if you are testing a training system, upload sample training courses for testers to take during UAT.

Input data can be included in test scripts or provided separately in a list or spreadsheet by test case that references what data should be used in each script.

For any test case or test script, the data that need to be available for that test is a precondition so we have to consider all the test data at test design. The earlier this is done the better because making up user accounts and populating them with data for testing may be time-consuming and it will need support from specialists who may not be available at short notice.

Depending on the data requirements for UAT the data available in the system may be previous test data, standard production data or a copy of data from a live environment. Data can also be created during one test script that supports later test scripts. If a script requires the UA tester to create a new account for example, a later test script may need the tester to log in to an existing account for which the details of the account that was previously created may be used. Standard production data are unlikely to suffice completely unchanged and some test-specific data will probably need to be added.

If the requirements include a check of the performance of the system, you will require a large data set. If the system acquires data from or updates data to a large database, then a large data volume plays an important role while testing the system for performance. Clearly a system with very little data in it will perform these tasks more quickly, all things being equal, than a system with a lot of data. If you need real-time data that are impossible to create manually, then you could ask the project manager to make them available from the live environment. If this is not possible, some performance tests should already have been carried out as part of system testing that may provide reassurance to the business representatives about the performance of the system.

One tempting source of data is the live environment but be aware that using copies of live data or the live environment can infringe the Data Protection Act, compromise commercially sensitive information and represent a significant risk to the organisation. If use of live data is being considered it will need approval at the highest level, and even if approved the security of the data must be paramount:

- Is encryption in place that protects the database?
- Will you know whether test data has been compromised?
- Who is responsible for securing test data?
- Does the data contain sensitive staff or client information?

Even if all these questions can be answered satisfactorily remember that if real data is displayed during testing, even when the database is encrypted, it can be downloaded or copied using a simple screen grab. If it is crucial to UAT that real data is used and its use is approved, data masking can be used to retain the data's properties yet create new, depersonalised, data. Finally, remember that the transfer of live data could overwrite any manually created test data.

What defines good test data?

The perfect test data are the smallest data set that allows UAT to identify all the errors in the system. Test data should obviously incorporate all the aspects of the system being tested but not exceed cost and time constraints for preparing test data and running tests. The exception to this rule is where it is quicker to use a copy of the live environment than to create test data from scratch or from the standard production data, in which case there may be more data than needed but the provision of this excess data has not affected project timescales or costs.

Preparing appropriate test data is a key part of UAT preparation. The test data set should be as close to perfect as possible in terms of cost and time.

What does a test script look like?

A completed test script will identify the test condition(s) and the test case(s) from which it was derived. It must also define the test precondition(s), input data, expected outcome and post-condition(s). Finally, it must incorporate the test data to be used in running the test, either embedded in the test script or in a file that is referenced from the test script.

Here is one example of what a test script might look like. There are many valid variations but a valid test script must include the details recorded in the example.

Example 7.6

An example test script
One of the requirements of Excelsior is that users can only access the parts of the system they are allowed to. Everyone in the company is able to access the HR module for instance, but only certain roles are allowed to access the Contracts module. This means the system needs to check that the person already logged on to Excelsior is on the list of those allowed access to the particular module they are trying to access. This is done using the system logon details.

1.2.1 Test scenario

1. Check an unverified user cannot log on to Contracts.
2. Check that a verified user can log on to Contracts.

Test scenario #1 – Check an unverified user cannot log on to Contracts.

Test step	Test description	Expected results	Pass ✓/Fail ✗
1.	From the Excelsior home page select the Contracts module	An error page should be displayed 'Access denied. You do not have permission to perform this action or access this resource. You can request access below' A 'Request Access' section on the screen will also be displayed	
2.	Close the error page displayed by selecting the X button in the top right corner of the screen	The home page should be displayed	

Test scenario #2 – Check a verified user can log on to Contracts.

Test step	Test description	Expected results	Pass ✓/Fail ✗
1.	From the Excelsior home page select the Contracts module	The Contracts home page should be displayed	

These are very short examples of the information that should be contained in a test script and may not be the most efficient when run in isolation.

Questions:

1. What other related testing do you think ought to be carried out?
2. As part of what other test scenarios could these tests be run?

Our answers can be found in Appendix B.

Example 7.7

A data input sheet
You can make the test data to be entered part of the test script so that the values to be entered are given in the test description column. However, if you would like the end-users to test a number of different values on the same screen, you can also consider providing a separate data input sheet to be used in conjunction with the test script. In the BVA example we used in this chapter you will probably want testers to attempt to enter 0, 1, 6 and 7 characters as part of the same test of the single field in order to save time. These values can be listed on a separate sheet that is used in conjunction with the test script. Data input sheets are also useful where a complex set of combinations of values need to be tested, for instance where a number of different types contract need to be tested that each contains different fields and needs to be accessible by different user roles. Keeping the data input values separate from the test scripts also gives you greater control over what is tested when the number of testers is reduced for instance, and saves having to extrapolate data from the missing tester's scripts. Note that, where possible, making end-users enter information based on real examples (but not using real data), customer or address details will add to the usefulness of testing.

Shaded areas indicate that the field does not need to be completed.

Table 7.5 A contract data input sheet

	Test step 1	Test step 2	Test step 3
Contract type	Turnover	Turnover	SOV
Minimum volume commitment			30,000

(Continued)

Table 7.5 (Continued)

	Test step 1	Test step 2	Test step 3
Goods sold in	Scotland England Wales Northern Ireland	Scotland	England Wales
Contact name	Pauline van Goethem	Use any contact information (but not real customer data)	Use any contact information (but not real customer data)
Contact street & no.	52 Salmond Place		
City	London		
County	Greater London		
Postcode	W1 5SQ		
Contract template type	Long form	Email	Short form

Note that a data input sheet can contain the data relevant per test script or can contain multiple entries that should be applied as part of the same test script. How the data input sheets should be used by the testers should be included in the UAT training.

CHAPTER SUMMARY

In this chapter we have demonstrated the hierarchy of test design in a practical way, taking the test basis for UAT and deriving from it test conditions, test cases and tests scripts and then adding the test data to enable the test scripts to be run. The techniques have been illustrated in examples and applied to our case study in the second step of a structured approach to UAT.

After reading this chapter you should be able to answer the following questions:

- How do I extract test conditions from the test basis?
- How do I create tests cases to verify test conditions?
- How do I select effective test cases to exercise different aspects of the system?
- How do I construct test scripts from test cases?
- How do I create test data to populate test scripts?

What have I learned?

Test your knowledge of Chapter 7 by answering the following questions. The correct answers can be found in Appendix B.

1. Traceability is important because:

   A. It links test conditions, cases and scripts back to the requirements
   B. It is a measure of risk
   C. It makes sure that the data for testing are complete
   D. It ensures each requirement has a unique ID

2. A test condition is:

   A. A condition that must be met for testing to take place
   B. A combination of features that are tested as part of a scenario
   C. A statement about a feature that can be verified by a test case
   D. An exit criterion for UAT

3. What **three** things should you be most aware of when it comes to test-case design?

   A. Have the requirements been covered?
   B. How many testers will there be?
   C. Do the cases cover the processes?
   D. Are the user interfaces being sufficiently tested?
   E. Which cases represent the greatest risk?

4. Which of the following is the most important reason for applying BVA?

   A. To keep the number of negative test cases to a minimum
   B. To identify all the negative test cases
   C. To identify the negative test cases most likely to uncover problems
   D. To identify the partitions between equal sets of data

Some questions to consider (our responses are in Appendix B)

1. The test cases have been created. When deciding what order they should be placed in, the project manager wants you to focus on risk and the project sponsor wants you to focus on processes. How do you decide what order they should be placed in?

2. On the first day of UAT half the team are off ill with a cold. What decision would you make about whether to run testing? What tests do you think you could run?

8 IMPLEMENTING THE TESTS

So far we have planned our UAT exercise and created an overall strategy for the testing, which we then followed up by designing all the tests and preparing test scripts. We are now ready to implement the plan and do the testing.

In this chapter we will explain how we schedule all the tests to achieve our test strategy and assess the system against the acceptance criteria. To do this we will need to log all the testing, so that we can determine when testing is complete, and collect the data we need to make a judgement about the system's status.

Topics covered in this chapter

- The testing schedule
- Implementing the test schedule
- Identifying progress
- The status report
- The post-testing summary

THE TESTING SCHEDULE

Test scheduling is just like any other scheduling; it puts activities in the right order and, ideally, estimates when each of them should happen.

Test schedule

A list of activities, tasks or events of the test process, identifying their intended start and finish dates or times, and interdependencies.

Test scheduling is actually a very important step because:

- It ensures that all the tests required by our test strategy are included.
- It sequences the tests for the most efficient use of time and resources.

- It sequences the tests to follow business processes.
- It allocates testing resources to testing activities.
- It enables us to log testing and keep track of progress.
- It enables us to reschedule if we hit problems.

Test scheduling is to test execution what the test plan is to our overall strategy; it turns the principles into hard reality that we can manipulate, track and modify. We know from experience that no plan is ever complete and nothing ever goes completely to plan. Test scheduling is our opportunity to maintain control of the testing project in the face of change and to ensure that we are always making the best use of the time and resources available to us.

The high-level test schedule

The purpose of the high-level schedule is to fit together the large 'building blocks' required by the test strategy into a sequence that works for our strategy and makes best use of the time and resources available.

The high-level test schedule is based directly on the UAT strategy. For example if the strategy is risk-based, the high-level schedule will schedule all the high-risk test items early. If it is based on relative importance, the most important features will be tested first.

Test scheduling has to take account of a number of different factors that will affect what can be tested when. These factors include:

- priority of tests;
- availability of a test environment;
- availability of testers.

Priority of tests

The priorities set by the UAT strategy determine the main sequence of testing but this may be amended by clashes in priority or by the unavailability of essential resources such as test environments and testers to run the tests.

Availability of a test environment

We need test environments to replace those parts of the real world or of the system to which we do not have access for some reason.

In some cases access to the real world is not feasible, for example a system that will operate interactively in real time across multiple time zones will require a complex, reliable and probably secure communications network. The network may already be in use or may not have been completed. In either case a test environment that duplicates the network would be impractical. A test environment may create a simulation of some aspect of the real world to enable testing or it may create a simplified version of the real hardware or software for testing. In the example either of these options may be too complex and costly, and some other alternative way of testing the system may have to be identified.

Where test environments are used throughout UAT there may be competition for the use of a given environment and testing will need to be scheduled to avoid or minimise the competition.

Availability of testers

Clearly testing requires testers to be available. It may be that specific skills or user background may be required for particular areas of testing and this will need to be taken into account when scheduling the tests.

> Nothing is guaranteed so scheduling is not a one-time exercise but a continuous review and rescheduling activity.

The detailed test schedule

The detailed test schedule takes the building blocks from the high-level schedule and breaks them down into individual tests. The scheduled flow of individual tests may, however, be interrupted by the status of the software under test (SUT) at each stage. If any test failure identifies a defect in the SUT, the sequence will break down. Figure 8.1 shows the life cycle of a test

Figure 8.1 The life cycle of a test

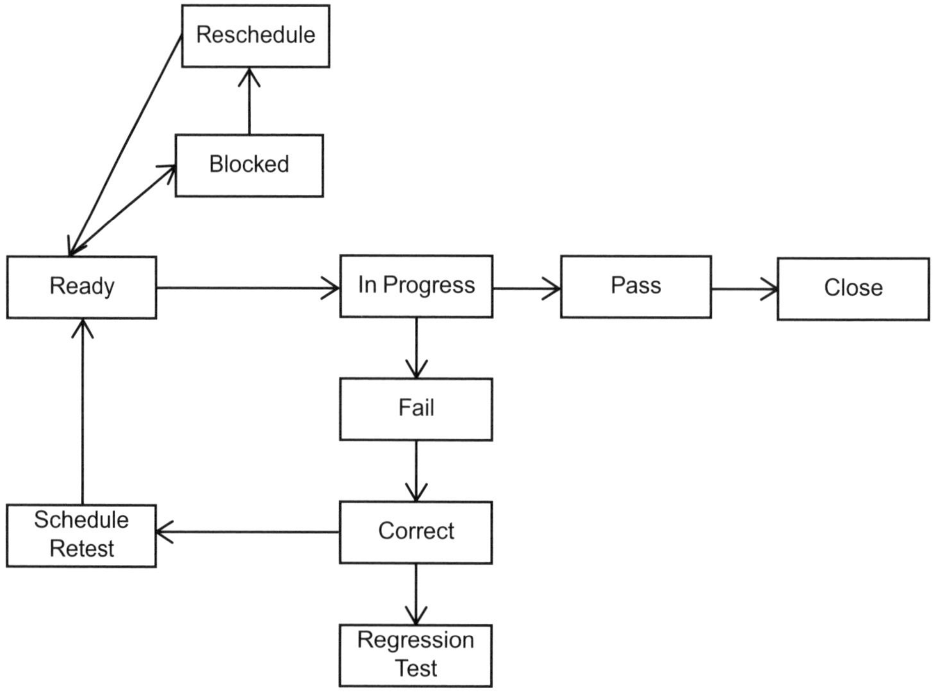

Status of the software under test (SUT)

The SUT is the specific area of the system being tested at any particular time or in any particular test. As testing progresses the focus will shift from one area of the system to another.

At any given stage there may be outstanding incident reports, or defects may be under investigation or correction. The availability of the SUT scheduled for a given time is therefore never certain. As far as possible, scheduling should take account of the expected availability of the specific area of the SUT for which tests are being scheduled.

Anything that knocks a test out of the queue to be tested affects the schedule in one way or another. Figure 8.1 demonstrates the ways in which a scheduled test may generate a reschedule:

- the need to reschedule if tests are blocked;
- the need to retest after defects have been corrected;
- the need for regression testing.

The need to reschedule if tests are blocked

If a serious defect is found there may be a need to prioritise the defect correction, and that may block tests that depended on having the defective module in place. It will also displace tests when the correction is scheduled for priority testing, necessitating a rejig of the schedule. There are many ways that a test can be blocked. When we have a block in our scheduled tests we have to reschedule to keep testing moving and fit the blocked test(s) in later.

The need to retest after defects have been corrected

Clearly any defects found are likely to lead to defect correction (though defect correction may be deferred if the defect is not too serious and the defect correction will not have a significant impact on completion of UAT). If defects are corrected, the correction will need to be tested; this will be testing that was not originally scheduled and so will necessitate some changes to the test schedules.

The need for regression testing

We can assume that some regression testing will be required during UAT but we cannot easily predict when. Two options are open to us: one is to plan a regression testing activity on a regular basis; the other is to do regression testing when it is required and reschedule around it.

Planned regression has the advantage that it does not cause rescheduling and, if no regression testing is required, it creates some 'slack' in the schedule that can absorb other reasons for change. The downside is that scheduled regression reduces the amount of time available for other testing. If we plan regression in as it is needed, we have to accept rescheduling of other tests, which may be inconvenient and may lead to delays. If we take this approach, we should assume that we will not complete all of the UAT initially planned (unless the timescale is extended) so we need to ensure the later tests are of relatively low priority or importance.

Streamlining

The detailed test schedule takes advantage of opportunities to streamline the testing by taking advantage of opportunities to sequence things in a natural order.

Here are some examples of streamlining:

- If the precondition of one test matches the post-condition of another, it may be advantageous to run these tests in sequence (even if the high-level schedule does not require that sequence). One good example is where test data are processed by test 1 into a form that test 2 needs as input.
- Where tests are time-sequenced it makes sense to keep them together.
- Where data input are required it makes sense to test the data input function at the same time. This could include error handling, even if error handling is notionally part of a block of testing that is scheduled separately.
- Business processes should not be separated into different parts of the schedule, even if one part of the process is a higher priority than another. The advantage of processing test data through the entire process and checking the output generally outweighs any disadvantages of adjusting the schedule to make the process fit.

The detailed test schedule will be a test-by-test sequence that provides the most efficient use of resources and provides the best visibility of the system behaviour within the overall constraints imposed by the UAT strategy. Table 8.1 is an example of a test schedule.

Exercise 8.1

In Chapter 7 we used an example of a test script (reproduced below for your convenience) and we know that test scripts can be created quickly when they cover the same process in different parts of the system, for instance logging on to each Excelsior module.

1.2.1 Test scenario

1. Check an unverified user cannot log on to Contracts.
2. Check that a verified user can log on to Contracts.

Table 8.1 Example of a test schedule
Excelsior UAT Test Schedule V1.0

Sequence number	Req'ment. no.	Module	Test case no.	Test case description	Input	Expected output	Test script ID	Tester	Process	Date completed
1.	S234	General Functionality - Security	GF–S1.54	Verify that the team member can log on to Excelsior	Team member 1 logon	Excelsior home page appears	SY1.5	PvG	New contract approval	
2.	S235	General Functionality - Security	GF–S1.54	Verify that team manager can log on to Excelsior	Team manager 1	Excelsior home page appears	SY2.3	BH	New contract approval	
3.	NC6	Excelsior - Contracts	C – N1.2	Create a new third-party contract	Contract details Contract Type: Third-party Address details: Use real customer IR35?: No Flexible Contract Terms: No Country: GB	Contract is created containing the pertinent clauses	CT3.3	PvG	New contract approval	
4.	NC7	Excelsior - Contracts	C – N1.2	Send third-party contract for approval	New contract created in step 3	Contract is received by team manager	CT3.4	PvG	New contract approval	
5.	NC7	Excelsior - Contracts	C – N1.3	Team manager approves a third-party contract	Approve contract sent for approval in step 4	Contract is approved and sent for signature	CT3.5	BH	New contract approval	

Test script #1 – Check an unverified user cannot log on to Contracts.

Test step	Test description	Expected results	Pass ✓/Fail ✕
1.	From the Excelsior home page select the Contracts module	An error page should be displayed 'Access denied. You do not have permission to perform this action or access this resource. You can request access below' A 'Request Access' section on the screen will also be displayed	
2.	Close the error page displayed by selecting the X button in the top right corner of the screen	The home page should be displayed	

Test script #2 – Check a verified user can log on to Contracts.

Test step	Test description	Expected results	Pass ✓/Fail ✕
1.	From the Excelsior home page select the Contracts module	The Contracts home page should be displayed	

Using the same example but applying it to the task of scheduling, do you think:

1. These tests should be scheduled in sequence, one following the other?
2. They could be run as part of another scenario or scenarios and, if so, which ones?

Our answers can be found in Appendix B.

IMPLEMENTING THE TEST SCHEDULE

Implementation is about assigning activities from the detailed test schedule to individual testers and ensuring that they have the necessary test scripts and test environments in place. Testers then set up and run their tests according to the test script, identifying any difficulties by annotating the test script, noting down the exact results and raising an incident report if the test does not produce the expected output.

Allocating tasks

Testing tasks may be allocated on a 'first come, first served' basis where any available tester takes on the next scheduled test script, or test scripts may be annotated for execution by testers from a particular specialism, for example end-users, managers or business analysts.

Once tasks are allocated the tester is expected to locate the appropriate test script(s) and the workstation at which the test is to be executed.

Executing test scripts

Testers set up the test as defined in the test script and run the script with any test data specified for the test.

If a test passes, the tester completes the input and output data and any other output events then adds the test result to the test script. If a test fails, the tester will raise an incident report and let the UAT team leader know what has happened.

All testing activity is entered by the UAT team leader onto the test log.

Logging the tests

The test log is initially a copy of the detailed test schedule onto which information is added to indicate who ran each test, when it was run, what the result was and so on. Table 8.2 provides a simple example of a test log.

The test log is a 'living' document. Information is added to it continually as tests are completed, and new activities are created as necessary to accommodate the following:

- Incidents are reported, defects are corrected and retesting is required.
- Tests are rescheduled because of delay or lack of resources.
- Tests are rescheduled around retesting.
- Regression testing is added.
- Feedback from testing identifies that additional or reduced testing is required.

The schedule identifies what testing has still to be done at any stage and the test log identifies what testing has been done. From the two documents we can determine where we are with respect to the schedule and with respect to the acceptance criteria. We can also derive other valuable test metrics such as the numbers of incidents raised and closed, and average times for testing. These will help us to refine our estimates of when we will complete UAT.

Raising issues from UAT

If a test cannot be completed satisfactorily for any reason, the UAT team leader should be consulted to resolve the problem.

Contracts

Purchase Orders

Training

Payments

Self-service HR

Total	0	0%	0	0	0

Table 8.2 Example of a test log

Issue no.	Test script ID	Tester	Step no.	Date raised	Module tested	Test case description	Defect description	Defect severity 1–3	Repeated	In scope	Assigned to	Issue resolution status
1.	SY1.5.6	KD	8	2.5.13	General Functionality – Security	The user has the ability to reset their password from the login screen	Reset screen does not recognise old password details. Error message: 'Password not recognised' on clicking Reset button.	2	Every time	Y	AndyF	Retest
2.	CS4.5.13	JD	3	2.5.13	Contracts	The user logs on with the Contracts Manager role	Correct Username: contractsmanager1 and Password: UAT are not accepted. Error message: 'Invalid user details' on clicking logon button.	3	Every time	Y	BrianH	Complete

(Continued)

Table 8.2 (Continued)

Issue no.	Test script ID	Tester	Step no.	Date raised	Module tested	Test case description	Defect description	Defect severity 1–3	Repeated	In scope	Assigned to	Issue resolution status
3.	TG3.5.16	AmG	14	2.5.13	Training	User can save an online training course to finish at a later date	Training course when reselected has not retained previous answers. No option appears to resume course.	2	One time	Y	JonL	In Progress
4.	TG3.12.5	KD	7	2.5.13	Training	User opens an online training course	Incorrect field label: Coure Name should be Course Name.	3	N/A	N	JonL	In Progress
5.	SR1.3.14	KD	22	1.5.13	Self-service HR	User updates address details	User can access other HR details including address details from this screen. Admin menu options are available.	1	Every time	Y	AndyF	In Progress
6.												
7.												
8.												

Minor   Retest

Major   In Progress
            Complete

Figure 8.2 Example of an incident report

Excelsior System	UAT	Incident No.

Incident Report

Incident Date/Time: 01/05/2013 14:27

Tester: B Hambling   **Contact Details:** 020 8554 ****

Logon: TeamManager1

Test Script ID: 3.12.1

Incident Severity: High

Repeatable?: Yes – Every time

Incident Description:

1. Module name/Number: General functionality - user interface

2. Script procedure step where incident occurred: Step 3

3. Point of failure (e.g. screen number): Signed screen

4. Description of incident (please give details of any error messages and actual and expected results)

Expected
On clicking the Approve Contract link from the Signed screen the Approve Contract screen should open and the selected contract should appear.

Actual
On clicking the Approve Contract link from the Signed screen the following error dialogue box appears: 'Error 26004. Could not start EXE Service in CTX_EXE_ StartEXEService State = 1' Dialogue box has OK button, which when pressed closes dialogue, does not appear to have any other effect.

5. Retest

When link is clicked again the same error message appears. When link next to other contracts is clicked the same error message appears. Repeated test with the other two Team Manager logons (2&3) at 14:45 and 14:53. All have the same issue. Test not repeated with the other user logons as the link does not appear on the equivalent Signed screens.

6. Special Circumstances: None

7. Signature

B. Hambling

If the test executes correctly but produces an output that is different from the expected output on the test script, an incident report should be raised. Where possible it is always prudent to attempt to rerun the test to confirm that the test was correctly set up and executed, but this is not always possible (for example if data have been changed and cannot be reset). If the problem relates to an error in the test case or the test script, the documentation will need to be amended and the test rescheduled. Figure 8.2 provides an example of a simple incident report.

Completed incident reports should be handed to the UAT team leader for evaluation and onward transmission to the development team.

Evaluating the importance of issues

The relative importance of incidents will depend on the severity of the incident and the anticipated impact on testing. The severity of an incident is usually based on guidelines set by the project manager in conjunction with users. Severity relates to the impact of the defect on the system and therefore the impact on the business when the system is in operation. Therefore a high-severity incident is typically one that threatens the viability of a key business process being supported by the system. The impact on testing will depend to some extent on severity (because a high-severity incident may halt testing while an investigation is carried out) but also on the other testing that is going on in related areas of the system. The UAT team leader needs to communicate the relative priority of the incident as far as UAT is concerned so that defect corrections can be prioritised to minimise the impact on UAT progress as well as correcting the most serious defects as early as possible.

IDENTIFYING PROGRESS

The test log identifies what testing has been done and what the outcomes were. The test schedule summarises what still remains to be done for UAT – we cannot identify exactly what remains to be completed because we do not know what defects might still be present in the software. Trend information from the test schedule and test log can be very helpful in this estimation.

Progress against schedule

Progress against schedule is a measure of how much of the scheduled testing has been completed to date. If we had expected to complete half of the tests on a certain date and the test log indicates we have completed less than half then we are behind schedule. How far we are behind will depend on why we have been delayed. A delay caused by unavailability of a test environment or of testers may not have any knock-on effect, provided the reason for unavailability is not likely to cause further delays. A delay caused by defect corrections and retesting is likely to have a greater effect. Metrics related to the number and severity of defects found, the average times taken to correct and retest, and the subsequent average impact on the test schedule will provide a basis for estimating the future impact of defects, though we will have to either assume that the defect rate will stay the same as it was in the first half of testing or estimate how it might change in the second half.

Accurate estimation of delay in a situation where defect counts are relatively high is difficult, but this is not a situation we would normally expect to apply to UAT. It is more likely that the start of UAT will have been delayed because of defect corrections during system testing or even earlier in the development life cycle. Wherever delay originates, though, it needs to be assessed and projected onto the remaining part of the schedule so that the project manager is aware of the potential delay to project completion.

Progress against acceptance criteria

Progress against acceptance criteria will depend on what the criteria are. For illustration we assume that the main criteria were related to test coverage and defects outstanding on completion of UAT.

Test coverage is directly measurable and the tests would have been designed to achieve the required level of coverage, so completion of the tests for which coverage is being tracked will provide a measure of progress against this criterion. If coverage is not being tracked directly, we should be able to see what tests remain to be completed to achieve the required coverage.

Progress against defect counts is harder to assess but the history will inform us. If defect counts have been high so far, we should expect them to remain high and estimate completion accordingly. If defect counts have so far been very low, we can reasonably assume they will stay low and estimate little or no delay to the scheduled completion date.

Adding up the potential delays associated with each of the acceptance criteria will provide us with an overall estimate of completion that can be combined with the estimate of completion of scheduled tests. The estimates cannot be expected to be accurate to within hours or even a day or so, but we should be able to determine whether or not we expect to be delayed in completing UAT.

THE STATUS REPORT

The UAT status report is a summary of all our progress information, our estimates of when we expect to complete UAT and our recommendations with data to support them. Figure 8.3 suggests some headings for a brief test summary report. In a small UAT exercise this may be as simple as a spreadsheet with commentary. In a large UAT project lasting weeks, it may be a formal report delivered on a regular, perhaps weekly, basis.

The status report lays out for the project manager our measurements and the basis of our estimates so that they can determine whether any anticipated delay is acceptable. If not, some form of compromise will need to be sought.

At this stage we cannot expect to be able to remedy any fundamental weaknesses in the system before release so the choice comes down to relaxing acceptance criteria, postponing the delivery date or both.

THE POST-TESTING SUMMARY

On completion of UAT, or when we are directed to stop testing, we will need to produce a report that contains all of the summary information up to the end of UAT and provides an accurate assessment of the status of the system. That evaluation will be the subject of Chapter 9.

Figure 8.3 Example status report contents

Excelsior UAT Test Summary Report

Date:

Overview (outline of testing performed since the last report)

Summary Assessment
      Tests planned
      Tests run
      Tests passed
      Tests failed
      Tests blocked
      Incidents reported
      Incidents resolved

Progress to Date
      Tests run/total tests
      %age tests passed
      %age tests failed
      %age coverage achieved
      Tests still to be run
      Incidents unresolved

Status Against Plan
      %age tests complete
      Schedule slippage
      Schedule status
            Tests outstanding
            Blocked tests
            Regression tests outstanding

Status Against Acceptance Criteria
      %age tests complete
      %age requirements coverage achieved
      Defects outstanding
            Critical
            Serious
            Routine

Recommendations (any changes proposed to enhance progress/quality of testing)

Signature: **Date:**

> **CHAPTER SUMMARY**
>
> This chapter has addressed the practical issues of running tests, logging issues and evaluating progress. The importance of consistent process and accurate reporting cannot be overemphasised and we will be rewarded by the ability to pinpoint issues needing resolution and clarity about where we are in relation to our acceptance criteria.
>
> After reading this chapter you should be able to answer the following questions:
>
> - What does a test schedule tell me?
> - What should I log when I run a test?
> - What should I report if I spot an issue?
> - How do we discover where we are in relation to our acceptance criteria?
> - What should go into summary reports to stakeholders?
> - How often should I report?

What have I learned?

Test your knowledge of Chapter 8 by answering the following questions. The correct answers can be found in Appendix B.

1. What should be done by the UAT leader immediately after a tester discovers a defect?
   - **A.** Check the test script is not the cause of the fault
   - **B.** Attempt to recreate the defect
   - **C.** Ensure the defect has been logged in enough detail and the severity has been established
   - **D.** All of the above

2. A test failed because of a mistake in the script. What do you do?
   - **A.** Raise an incident report
   - **B.** Do not raise an incident report; amend the script and run it again
   - **C.** Do not raise an incident report; amend the script and schedule it for future testing
   - **D.** Raise an incident report, amend the script and run it again

3. What does the test log record?
   - **A.** How much time is needed to complete the remaining testing
   - **B.** What testing has been completed and the outcomes
   - **C.** Incidents and their severity
   - **D.** What testing has been completed

A question to consider (our response is in Appendix B)

1. Halfway through testing you are asked to provide a fixed date for finishing UAT. What would your answer to this request be?

9 EVALUATING THE SYSTEM

One thing that should be clear by now is that what is 'acceptable' is a very hard concept to pin down. In the case of an IS it depends on how the system was built or acquired, who the stakeholders are and what their needs are. There is no 'one size fits all' answer to the question. What we need to understand and be able to apply is a process for determining whether a particular system is acceptable in a particular scenario, and that is what this chapter will focus on.

This chapter is about the final decision to accept or not accept a system. In practice, of course, the decision is not simple and nor does it have only two possible outcomes. There is a range of possible scenarios that we will explore, each relating to whether and to what extent the acceptance criteria have been demonstrably met.

Topics covered in this chapter

- How do we decide whether or not to accept a system?
- When the testing has to stop
- The risk of release
- Measuring the risk of release
- Defining and evaluating emergency-release criteria
- Decision process for evaluating UAT results
- Test summary report conclusions
- The final release decision

HOW DO WE DECIDE WHETHER OR NOT TO ACCEPT A SYSTEM?

The simple answer is that we have to decide whether or not the system has met its acceptance criteria, but that answer assumes we have a neat package of criteria that we can assess. If you have taken the advice in this book to heart and applied it to your project, you should have a set of criteria to work with; if not, you will need a practical and pragmatic decision process.

Figure 9.1 presents the logic of acceptance in its simplest form.

Figure 9.1 Process for deciding go/no go for release

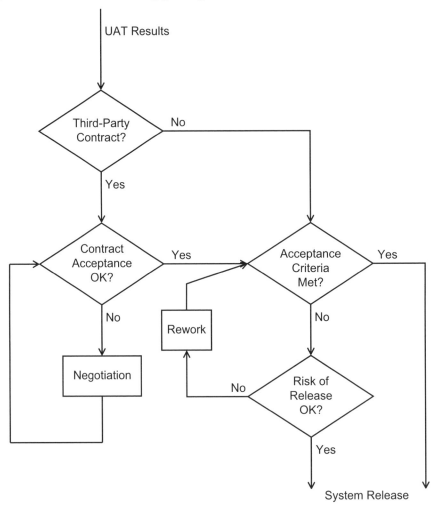

The logic contains four decisions, of which three are key to acceptance.

Decision 1 is about whether or not the development was contracted to a third party or, equivalently from an acceptance standpoint, whether or not the system was acquired from a third-party supplier. In either case there will be some contractual criteria on which final payment is based. This is not the same thing as acceptance of the system but it is a necessary prerequisite.

Decision 2 assumes that there are contractual criteria and asks whether or not they have been met. If we find the contractual criteria have been met, the supplier must be paid and we have to work with what has been delivered. If not, we would expect to enter some kind of negotiation with the supplier that will result in a settlement that improves the situation from our point of view. The key factor here is the relationship of the contract criteria to the acceptance criteria set by the stakeholders. There is unlikely to be a perfect fit unless the system was specially custom-built to meet your exact requirements, in which case the contract criteria and the acceptance criteria will be the same. In most cases the contract criteria will relate to the computer system that is at the heart of the IS but not the IS itself. We will still need to ensure that the IS as a whole meets our business need and is acceptable to our user community, and that will usually mean more testing and more work to achieve an acceptable release, and there will still be two more decisions to take.

Decision 3 asks whether the system achieves its acceptance criteria, which implies that the business benefits for which it was built or acquired can be achieved. For contracted systems, achievement of contract criteria leads on to this decision; for systems built in-house we arrive at this as the first acceptance decision. Remember that acceptance criteria are pragmatic and take into account both the business value of the system and the risk of releasing it. Achieving the acceptance criteria means that we now have a platform on which to build up the business value so we can take the step of releasing it. We need to bear in mind, however, that there may still be quite a lot of work to do to ensure the system as released is capable of growing business value to achieve the business benefits for which it was originally commissioned. Release of the system does not guarantee that the benefits will be achieved and a plan for ramping up the value of the system to the business will still be a priority.

Decision 4 is the fallback question and the one that needs to be exercised much more often than it is; it asks whether the risk of releasing the system is acceptable. All the information we have gathered will be needed to get a sound answer to this question, and all the stakeholders will need to be ready and willing to engage in a serious assessment of the possible outcomes if the system is released. This is an ideal opportunity to use some kind of scenario analysis to identify what could happen after release and assess how the system in its current state would cope, looking beyond the immediate boundary of the system to the business effects of any shortfall in performance or capability. Development of scenarios for this risk assessment would be a good opportunity for the users, developers, managers and sponsor(s) to work as a team. The work of scenario building will be valuable even if the system proves to meet all its acceptance criteria, but it will be absolutely priceless if it does not and will speed up the process of making the system fit for use.

WHEN THE TESTING HAS TO STOP

We began with a clear idea about how much testing we would need to do and an equally clear idea about how we would determine whether the system was fit to release to its users. That framework enabled us to plan and execute structured testing and gather data about the status of testing and the state of the system. Once our plan has been completed and all the data gathered, we can stop testing and evaluate the results to decide whether or not to accept the system.

That is an ideal scenario, of course, and one that we cannot expect to be the reality we face at the end of our UAT project; we need to be ready for alternative scenarios. Among these might be:

- The business can no longer afford to burn money on the project and needs to get the system into service.

- The benefits of the system are time-critical and time is running away.

- The testing is finding few, if any, problems and further testing is hard to justify.

These are realistic scenarios and the challenge for us is how to react to them. Our approach must enable us to evaluate the system at any stage in testing so that none of these scenarios catches us unprepared. That is one reason why routine reporting on the testing was recommended and, as part of that reporting, a regular update of progress towards the acceptance criteria so that we have a clear idea of where we are in relation to the release decision at every stage in testing.

Therefore the first and most important lesson is that evaluation of the system must be continuous and consistent. That is to say we must decide how we will evaluate the system and set up the processes of evaluation from the beginning so that we can, at any stage, produce a credible evaluation of the state of the system.

If we do have to stop testing before it is completed, for any reason, we will need to evaluate the risk of release and the business value of the system in its current state.

THE RISK OF RELEASE

All the work we did at the planning stage was leading up to this challenge. We put in place acceptance criteria to make the decision on fitness for release as objective as possible. We set targets for test coverage and levels of defects that provided us with clear visibility of the status of the system at each stage. If all our criteria have been met, we have no difficulty in making a decision to accept the system.

But what if the criteria have not been met when testing is complete? And what if the criteria have still not been met when testing has to stop? These are the most important questions we have to answer.

The answer, in a word, is risk. We have to decide what the level of risk is in releasing a system that is not ready according to our criteria. What is the probability that it will fail partially or completely, and what would be the consequences of failure? This is the reason we decided at the outset that risk-based testing would be a good approach. With risk-based testing we have confidence that every test reduces the risk by some amount and, however tiny the reduction of risk might be, it will be accumulating day by day and test by test. If we have tested using a risk-based approach, we can at least say that the risk of release is as low as we could make it on the day the decision has to be made.

But whether we have been using a risk-based approach or not does not change the need to be able to make a decision about the risk that remains in releasing the system at a given time and at a given stage in the testing.

We need to make a judgement based on the best data we have available and centred around acceptance criteria. The actual evaluation will depend on the criteria we set initially, but we can define a process that will work in every case.

MEASURING THE RISK OF RELEASE

Turning again to Figure 9.1 we can see that there are two ends to the risk spectrum. If we have prepared the way by carefully defining contractual or acceptance criteria at the start of the project and we have maintained control of all incidents, defects and other changes during the project, the final decision is very likely to be clear-cut and the risk of release is likely to be small. We could still have built the wrong system for the business purpose or diverged from our original intent in some way, but the monitoring of our progress will have shown up these problems at a relatively early stage. We may have a hard decision to make about whether to release – hard in the sense of being unpopular and uncomfortable – but we should have an easy decision in the sense that the correct or best (most appropriate) outcome will be easy to determine. The purpose of this whole process has been to make rational decisions possible and this will have been achieved, even if the outcome is not the one originally desired.

If, on the other hand, we have not defined contract or acceptance criteria at the outset or we have not monitored the development and testing process carefully so that we have a continuously updated record of the quality of the outputs and the status of the system in terms of defects and incidents at this stage, then we have a hard decision to make – this time hard in the sense that it will not be easy to reach a sound conclusion from the information available.

What follows will therefore consider the latter scenario. How do we proceed if we have no clear criteria for acceptance? What can we do to enable a rational decision in the face of incomplete and possibly conflicting information and with business and time pressures militating against spending time on gathering and assessing data? Remember that as UA testers we are not the decision makers, but we are closest to the system at this point and therefore best able to identify risk factors and report to decision makers in a way that is helpful, positive and constructive – always remembering that we will also be the last group to touch the system before release, so we will be remembered as being at least partially responsible for the outcome.

DEFINING AND EVALUATING EMERGENCY-RELEASE CRITERIA

If we have no positive acceptance criteria to identify what we want from the system, we have to fall back on some more defensive criteria to try to protect ourselves from trouble. There are three parameters that will be of some value to us in this decision:

1. stability of the system;
2. usability of the system;
3. coverage of the testing.

Stability

Stability is a measure of a system's ability to cope with change. We need the system to be stable enough for us to put in place an improvement plan that will almost certainly involve changes to the computer system at the heart of the IS. If the computer system cannot accommodate change, we will be unable to improve it to meet our original expectations.

We must at least ensure we understand how stable the system is so that we have confidence that we can make essential changes to improve its business value, performance, usability or other parameters as we need to.

Measuring stability

One way to assess stability is to look at what changes have been made during development, why they were made and what problems, if any, arose after changes were made. To do this we would need to review the incidents that have been raised, the defects that were identified and corrected, and the changes that were made as the system was built. The testing logs will confirm whether the planned changes were stable and the IM system will tell us whether changes made to correct defects resulted in a clean new release or the discovery of further defects.

If we have access to incident logs and change logs, we can identify the relationship between changes and defects and see whether changes tended to cause spikes in defect rates. This is a typical pointer to instability.

Usability

Usability is defined here in a very informal way as a measure of how well the users can operate the computer system at the heart of the IS. If users have difficulty in using the system effectively, improvements will be hard to make because users will be trying to interface with a system that is already problematical for them; change could make matters considerably worse.

Determining usability

What we are seeking here is an informal but reliable assessment of how well users will be able to manage to operate the system to deliver at least basic services while the improvement programme is being implemented. A good mechanism would be to define a core set of user interactions that enable key services, provide a broad range of user interactions and create a scenario that users can work through in a consistent way. A small but representative group of trained end-users can then work through the scenario and provide feedback on their experience. Each user should be timed as they work through the scenario and feedback should be via a standard questionnaire or an interview with structured questions. Defining the scenario and the feedback mechanism would be a good exercise for end-users, managers and sponsor(s) to tackle as a team. Users will need to be well briefed so that they are not intimidated by the exercise.

The results should provide a good guide to the system's usability as perceived by its users and the exercise will have the additional benefit of engaging the end-user community in the improvement programme from the outset.

Coverage

We have already defined coverage of testing as a measure of how much of the system has been tested so far. The measures of stability and usability must be viewed against coverage because a system that is unstable or unusable when, say, only 25 per cent of the requirements have been tested is facing major rework. At the other end of the spectrum, a system that has been tested against 90 per cent of the requirements and is reasonably stable and usable represents a low risk as a platform for improvement.

We need to seriously consider the testing we have done throughout the life cycle and in UAT and decide whether it is enough on which to base any decision.

Determining test coverage

If we have not designed tests to achieve specific levels of test coverage, we can still make some attempt to identify what has been tested in the test cases that have been run. We first need to analyse some test cases to determine how they relate to requirements. This needs to be done by a testing specialist, a business analyst or a developer; it may require skills and insights we could not reasonably expect an end-user to have and we need this exercise done quickly. Once the sample analysis is completed we may have a simple way to determine requirements coverage for the whole UAT suite. We may find that requirements coverage is high, in which case the testing has been quite effective. If we find coverage is low, there should be some concern about possible undiscovered defects in important areas.

If the initial analysis cannot determine coverage, for example if tests have been constructed without reference to requirements, we can only draw the conclusion that requirements coverage is very low. This is, in itself, not necessarily a barrier to an improvement programme, but it points to potential problems ahead and it certainly identifies a gap that must be filled as part of the improvement programme – the achievement of systematic testing to provide coverage data for the future as changes are made.

Determining whether emergency criteria have been met

Using all the data about incidents, defects, changes, usability and coverage that we can find, we should be able to draw some conclusions about risk of release. The data may not allow detailed conclusions but it would be unusual to find that this brief investigation did not lead to a conclusion that risk of release was relatively high or relatively low, and that may be enough for our purposes.

These three criteria are our emergency fallback. They are in no sense an alternative to more rigorous acceptance criteria because all they provide us with is a measure of the confidence we can have that the computer system is a suitable platform for making incremental improvements. This is a last-ditch effort to keep the system alive while we work out a plan to enhance it to the level we originally anticipated and paid for.

DECISION PROCESS FOR EVALUATING UAT RESULTS

We now have a generic process for drawing conclusions about the outcome of UAT. The level of detail and the firmness of conclusions will depend on the extent and quality of testing done and the detail of records that have been kept, but the approach will be similar in each case.

Step 1 – contract acceptance

If, and only if, there was an external contract to build our system, or if a system was acquired with or without modification, there are certain to be criteria associated with acceptance of the system from the supplier(s). These criteria are likely to be similar in kind to those we define for our own acceptance decision and they should be measurable so that determination of acceptance is clear-cut and not open to debate. Step 1 is to evaluate these criteria (or that part of the criteria that relates to testing) and report the results to the relevant stakeholders with a recommendation whether to accept or not.

The process cannot proceed to the next step until this one is complete, so any discrepancies or negotiations need to be completed before we can move on to step 2.

If there was no third-party contractual involvement in development, the process moves on to step 2.

Step 2 – meeting acceptance criteria

Our own acceptance criteria were based on the extent to which business intent has been achieved. These, too, should be measurable and relatively straightforward to evaluate. We should have been tracking how far we are from achieving these criteria throughout UAT, so this final evaluation should not require major activity. It should yield a clear determination of whether or not the system meets its business intent and this should be reported to the relevant stakeholders with a recommendation. This is usually in the form of a UAT completion report that describes exactly what testing has been done for UAT and the results of that testing in relation to the acceptance criteria. Figure 9.2 is an outline of a UAT completion report.

In the event that acceptance criteria are not met, a decision by the stakeholders will require some input from the UAT team so we need to ensure that the UAT completion report incorporates an assessment of the performance of the system against each of the acceptance criteria, identifies how far the system is from achieving the criteria and assesses the implications of any gaps. Based on this analysis the report should suggest possible alternative courses of action for the stakeholders to consider.

Step 3 – assessing risk of release

Whenever acceptance criteria are not met we should carry out an assessment of the risk of releasing the system in its current state. The mechanism for this was outlined in step 2, but if data related to acceptance criteria are limited we can use the approach outlined in the section 'Defining and evaluating emergency-release criteria'. Our conclusions in this case will typically be more tentative than those associated with a clear evaluation of acceptance criteria and, consequently, more commentary will normally be needed to enable the stakeholders to make their own evaluation of the possible outcomes and the risks associated with each of them so that they can make a release decision.

Figure 9.2 UAT completion report format

UAT Completion Report Outline

Introduction

Purpose of the document
Identification of system under test
Scope of UAT

Overview

Outline the test process, testing activities, environments, software releases, time period, participants.

Acceptance Criteria

Identify individual criteria and the levels set for acceptance.

Constraints

Any constraints on testing related to e.g. environments, resource availability.

Test Results Summary

Overall summary of tests planned and run, passed and failed. Tests not run or failed test not yet resolved.

Test Incidents Summary

Overall summary of tests incidents raised and resolved by severity. Unresolved test incidents.

Acceptance Criteria Evaluation

Details of evaluation for each criterion.

Overall Assessment

Overall assessment of all acceptance criteria against requried levels.

Recommendations

Recommendations related to release or risk reduction prior to release.

Appendices

Detailed Test Results
Test Incident Reports

TEST SUMMARY REPORT CONCLUSIONS

The conclusions in the UAT completion report will need to be structured around the extent to which business intent has been achieved and the level of risk associated with releasing the system. We can identify a range of possible recommendations at this point.

Outcome 1 – release the system as it is

This is the most optimistic outcome. It implies that business benefits have been met and the risk of release is low. There may be some discrepancies in acceptance criteria but these are not significant enough to require any specific action.

Outcome 2 – defer release until key risk reduction measures are in place

Outcome 2 implies that business benefits have not been fully achieved and that risk of release is relatively high. Recommendations on risk reduction activities can also be matched by activities to enhance the business benefits achievable by the system. If, for example, the number and severity of defects not yet corrected are considered high, the recommendation may be to defer release while this situation is improved. The improvement will take a certain amount of time and require a certain level of development resources, providing stakeholders with a spectrum of strategies to achieve more or less risk reduction in more or less time, using more or fewer resources. This allows other factors such as time or commercial pressures to be taken into account.

It would be prudent to measure stability and usability in this case to provide confidence that a risk reduction and improvement programme can be implemented without increasing the risk of a system failure.

Outcome 3 – release the system with additional support

Another option that can be considered is an immediate or early release but with additional resources committed to system support to offset the risk of early problems. This clearly depends on the nature of the expected problems and will be based on a risk analysis. Where the risk is related to possible user interface or performance problems that can be corrected within a reasonably short time frame, there may be an option to enhance the user support (for example by providing additional help resources and building FAQ lists from the test results to enable support staff to quickly diagnose problems and suggest effective 'workarounds').

As for outcome 2, there may be a spectrum of possible responses. Here, too, it would be prudent to measure stability and usability to provide confidence that a risk reduction and improvement programme can be implemented without increasing the risk of a system failure.

Outcome 4 – defer release and apply risk reduction and additional support

Outcome 4 is clearly a combination of outcomes 2 and 3. It becomes a serious alternative where there are risks associated with the system's ability to achieve its main functions, necessitating a deferment while risk reduction is taking place, and there are also potential issues related to the user interface or performance. The time spent on risk reduction is likely to require significant development resources so the less-critical defects will not be corrected in the short term. The additional support therefore eases the problems when the system is released after a deferment.

In this situation it would be important to evaluate the emergency-release criteria to ensure that the system can be brought to an acceptable standard in a realistic time frame and at reasonable cost.

Outcome 5 – reject the system

Outcome 5 is a logical possibility although it is unlikely to be an outcome at this stage because the feedback from development and testing would most likely have identified serious problems before this stage is reached.

THE FINAL RELEASE DECISION

The final release decision is in the hands of stakeholders and not the UAT team, but it is important for the UAT team leader to be available for consultation and advice. Whatever release decision is taken, the UAT team's results, data and experience are likely to be valuable in determining how to proceed to the next stage, whether that is an improvement programme or an immediate release of the system.

CHAPTER SUMMARY

This chapter has examined a range of possible scenarios at the end of UAT and for each of them it has identified an appropriate outcome and next steps.

After reading this chapter you should be able to answer the following questions:

- How can I be sure the system is ready for use?
- How do I know if the risk of releasing the software into service is manageable?
- Who decides if the system can be accepted?
- Who decides if the acceptance criteria have been met or not?
- What happens if the acceptance criteria are not fully met?
- What can we do to minimise risk if the acceptance criteria are partially met?

What have you learned?

Test your knowledge of Chapter 9 by answering the following questions. The correct answers can be found in Appendix B.

1. What are the **three** key decisions for acceptance?

    A. Was the build contracted to a third party?

    B. Is there an immovable deadline?

    C. Were there contractual criteria?

    D. Were the contractual criteria met?

    E. Does the system achieve the business benefits?

    F. Is the risk of releasing the system acceptable?

2. How can earlier UAT activities mitigate risk when testing has to finish early?

    A. Having taken a risk-based approach

    B. Having evaluated the UAT continuously

    C. Earlier UAT activities have no impact on mitigating risks during testing

    D. Both A and B are true

3. Which is the least likely outcome of the risk assessment?

    A. Release the system as it is

    B. Defer the release

    C. Release with extra support

    D. Do not release (reject the system)

Some questions to consider (our responses are in Appendix B)

1. The test manager wants to set up a meeting to discuss the release towards the end of UAT. Who should they invite and why?

2. There are a number of critical defects still outstanding. What does this mean in terms of the risk of release and to the release decision?

10 LIFE AFTER UAT

Once a decision to release a system has been made there is still much work to do to ensure a successful launch and, while those activities are beyond the scope of this book, we need to examine the large and important contribution that the outputs of UAT can make to that success. So this short chapter considers what happens after UAT.

Topics covered in this chapter

- Post-UAT reporting
- End-user training
- Preparing a roll-out strategy
- Implementation
- Post-implementation defect corrections
- Measuring business benefits
- The end of UAT?

POST-UAT REPORTING

After the UAT party is over there is serious work to be done. UAT is usually an activity that is completed against a backdrop of pressure, and completion is often a relief to all concerned. What happens next, though, can turn all the effort of UAT into a treasure house if the opportunity is grasped before the UAT team is disbanded and everything returns to normal.

Reporting may feel like a chore we would rather avoid but reporting on a well-planned and well-managed UAT gives us the opportunity to reflect on what has happened, gather and analyse the strands of information, and produce some powerful tools for the following phases.

There are many ways that a test summary report can be structured. Here is a simple outline of what a test summary report might contain so that we can explore what content it should have and how we might utilise that content to help with implementation, support, training and evaluation.

We repeat in Figure 10.1, for your convenience, the test completion report outline so that we can explore a little more detail to better understand what needs to be reported and why, and so that we can see what value this information can have for future phases of the system's life.

This is the format we used as the basis for decision making so it is designed to provide a succinct summary of the key information related to evaluation against acceptance criteria and evaluation of risk. We probably do not need all the collected data to draft this report but we do need to save them all because our need now is to look beyond the risk of release to the achievement of success, and for this we might need a revised structure to incorporate more analysis and evaluation.

Figure 10.2 is a report format that we can use as a forward-looking report. We can copy over all the relevant sections from the original test completion report so it is not a major effort to produce this, but the presentation of information is now slanted towards the activities still to be completed.

Most of the headings in the report should be self-explanatory but we will explore a little more the detail that can be covered in some of the sections.

Test reporting

Reporting on the tests should be simple enough. We have already established that enough testing was done to achieve the desired result but it still might be worth doing a little more analysis. Showing graphically how many tests passed and failed first time, how many passed after defect correction, how many passed and failed in different areas of the system and so on can be revealing. If you spot patterns or trends in the data, for example coverage was better in some areas than others or that test failures were more common in some areas than others, this is worth noting and following up.

The purpose of this report of the testing is to identify anything that might suggest there might be potential problems at implementation, so clustering is something to pay particular attention to.

Defects analysis

The starting point is graphical summaries again, this time of incidents raised and closed, defects identified and fixed, and both incidents and defects not yet closed. These will merit further investigation. It is interesting to look at incidents by age (how long they were open) because the longer-lived ones usually account for quite a lot of investigation or defect correction. We should also look at the rate of incidents being raised and closed. Spikes of incidents may point to spikes of testing activity or spikes of defects, so we should also report on the average incidents per test and significant deviations from that average. We might also look at defects per incident to see how many incidents were caused by other factors such as test script errors.

If we noted some clustering of test failures, we will see the same clustering in incident reports and here we can explore the clustering by areas of the system to see if there are areas where defect rates are higher than normal. These might be pointers to future problems. Closed incident reports will show the outcome, and in some cases this may

Figure 10.1 UAT completion report outline

UAT Completion Report Outline

Introduction

Purpose of the document
Identification of system under test
Scope of UAT

Overview

Outline the test process, testing activities, environments, software releases, time period, participants.

Acceptance Criteria

Identify individual criteria and the levels set for acceptance.

Constraints

Any constraints on testing related to e.g. environments, resource availability.

Test Results Summary

Overall summary of tests planned and run, passed and failed. Tests not run or failed test not yet resolved.

Test Incidents Summary

Overall summary of tests incidents raised and resolved by severity. Unresolved test incidents.

Acceptance Criteria Evaluation

Details of evaluation for each criterion.

Overall Assessment

Overall assessment of all acceptance criteria against requried levels.

Recommendations

Recommendations related to release or risk reduction prior to release.

Appendices

Detailed Test Results
Test Incident Reports

Figure 10.2 Post-UAT analysis report

Excelsior Post UAT Analysis Report

Introduction (Brief summary of the system purpose and key dates in implementation)

Purpose of the report

The main purpose is to analyse what happened in UAT and identify any pointers that can be used to smooth implementation.

Test Results Summary (graphical summaries of pass/fail, coverage etc.)

    Detailed Test Results

    Coverage Analysis

Incidents and Defects Summary (graphical summaries of incidents raised, defects by severity, etc.)

    Defects Analysis

    Unresolved Incidents

    Workarounds Identified

Support Summary

    Technical Support

    Business Support (Help)

Recommendations

    End-User Training

    User Guides

    Help System and FAQs

    Technical Support Issues

    Implementation Planning

    Risk Assessment

    Business Evaluation

Signature: **Date:**

have been a workaround rather than a change to the software. We may also have found some problems that required process changes and there may have been incidents that were reported several times by different people in different tests. Incidents that turn out to be duplicates can point to the kinds of problem that are hard to pin down and these might merit further attention.

Frequently asked questions (FAQs) and workarounds

The workarounds we identified from incident analysis can be documented as part of user training and documentation. FAQs can be distilled from individual tester's feedback and a workshop to debrief on the testing and shared experiences can be a useful way to capture these FAQs. They can be added to any online help and incorporated into end-user training and user guides.

Lessons learned

Lessons learned can take many forms. How could we have done UAT better? Did we have problems that could have been eliminated before UAT? Did we start UAT at the right time and were we prepared? Did we check on the entry criteria at the start of UAT? Did we meet the acceptance criteria at the end? Did UAT run to plan? If not, was the overrun in time, cost, effort or some combination? What caused the overruns? Could they have been avoided?

This is a list of questions that spring to mind. For a real lessons-learned session we should probably have a checklist of questions – some standard, some suggested by recent experience and some that will occur to us at the session. All the questions are worth answering because there may be patterns that will help us to avoid similar problems in future.

END-USER TRAINING

We can use the UAT training mechanism and materials as a starting point for end-user training, although we will need to take a slightly different perspective for end-users. All the previous analysis can be utilised to give end-users the best possible background on where to expect problems and how to deal with them, while the experience of UAT can be fed in with hints and tips on getting the best from the system. At least one part of the training could be delivered by a member of the UAT team to give end-users the opportunity to learn as much as they can from the experience of this person.

Training for new starters

New starters who arrive after the system is commissioned will need training and here again the insights from UAT can be helpful in 'grounding' the training.

PREPARING A ROLL-OUT STRATEGY

The evaluation of risk and subsequent analysis of UAT results and experience are important inputs into the roll-out strategy. Depending on the size and geographical spread of the organisation there might be a range of possible strategies, ranging from 'big bang' (putting the system on every desktop at once) to a series of pilot releases in different areas. Usually at least one pilot is used to enable any problems to be resolved in a relatively small implementation.

With the benefit of the UAT feedback a roll-out programme can be refined:

- High defect rates in UAT might suggest a smaller initial pilot followed by a ramp-up when problems have been identified and rectified.

- User interface problems might suggest a smaller pilot with increased support to help an initial group gain experience so that they can support a ramp-up.

- Workarounds can be trialled in a small initial pilot before the main roll-out.

- Revised user guides and help screens based on UAT feedback can be trialled in initial pilots.

- The absence of problems in UAT might encourage a slightly quicker ramp-up than had originally been envisaged.

IMPLEMENTATION

Full implementation, either initially or after a series of pilots, will still be a major stage in the life cycle. Feedback from UAT might be one way that required levels of technical support and business support (help desk) can be estimated for this exercise.

POST-IMPLEMENTATION DEFECT CORRECTIONS

Whatever happens during pilots or full implementation, some defects will emerge from the increased level of usage. Some of these defects will need to be corrected urgently, while others will be placed on the prioritised list of changes to be made over time.

If a collection of defect corrections is required in the early post-implementation period, there may need to be a new release of the system. Although this will be smaller than the original system release it will be critical because a system is already running and failures in the new release will therefore be critical to users, even if they are relatively minor. For that reason the option of reconstituting the UAT team to conduct a structured mini-UAT would be a good risk management strategy.

MEASURING BUSINESS BENEFITS

The final stage of full implementation is the ramp-up of the system to a level that will achieve the desired business benefits. This may come days, weeks or months after initial release depending on the level of problems that arise in the early period of use.

Unless the benefits are clear and obvious, for example providing a service that was not previously available, the business benefits will need to be measured to assure ourselves that they really have been achieved. Benefits such as improved profitability, reduced inventory or greater flexibility in the use of resources are the kinds of benefits that need a structured exercise of measurement.

Measurement can be done by analysing the data routinely collected by the system to identify expected changes, but this will take some time and will not eliminate the impact of other changes that might affect the measurement, for instance a period of bad weather that depresses sales. A more consistent result will need a controlled measurement exercise comparing the improvement parameters before and after the system is changed. The UAT team is an ideal resource for building the data by running the experimental data through the system before the changes are released and running it again at an agreed period after the changes have been released. The UAT team, with their recent experience of formal testing and the discipline of test reporting, would provide an ideal resource for the measurement exercise.

THE END OF UAT?

This final chapter has pointed to some of the ways that the UAT exercise and the experience and skills it develops in people can benefit other areas of the project and help to make implementation and evaluation easier and smoother.

The same set of skills and experience remains in the business after UAT and the unique experience of carrying out a structured test programme on an IS that brings important benefits to the business will have provided a major personal development opportunity for the team's members. As well as rewarding them for a job well done, it would be a good time to ensure that all these new skills and experience is recorded so that it can be called on again if and when a similar exercise is needed.

CHAPTER SUMMARY

This chapter has provided some guidance on what needs to happen during roll-out of the system you have tested. These are activities that are not the responsibility of the UAT team, but awareness is a valuable part of understanding 'the big picture' and may help you to do a better job of UAT.

After reading this chapter you should be able to answer the following questions:

- What happens after UAT is completed?
- How does a tested system get brought into service?
- What needs to be done to follow up on insights from UAT about system readiness?
- How can the organisation prepare itself for the new system's arrival?
- How can we minimise the risk of problems when we bring the system into service?
- How can we capture and harness the skills and experience gained during UAT?

APPENDIX A
UAT CHECKLISTS

1. Initiating the UAT Project (start of the development project)

2. Planning the UAT (as soon as agreed test basis deliverables are available for planning)

3. UAT Test Design (as soon as planning is complete)

4. UAT Test Execution (when the system is ready for test)

5. Release Decision (when the delivery was scheduled)

6. Post-UAT Actions (as soon as UAT is complete)

INITIATING THE UAT PROJECT CHECKLIST (SPONSOR)

1. Identify the key stakeholders (see page 29)

- by name and role
- agree responsibilities/accountability for the system
- agree business intent and objectives for the system
- agree resources to be made available for UAT

2. Select a team leader (see Chapter 4)

- decide selection criteria
- decide internal or external recruitment
- initiate selection process
- interview shortlist
- select a candidate

3. Communicate the business intent, objectives and acceptance criteria of the system (see Chapter 2)

- communicate the business intent, objectives and acceptance criteria to the team leader

4. Agree on the UAT team resources (see Chapter 4)

- team size and expertise
- accommodation
- test environments
- tools
- training

5. Agree on documentation to support UAT (see Chapters 2 and 6)

- RS
- business processes
- user expectations
- any need to gather user stories/use cases
- test management tools/processes
- version control
- IM
- test logging
- test reporting

6. Agree on decision making structures (see Chapter 9)

- decision making process at delivery
- authority for release decision
- information required to enable decision making
- acceptance criteria
- quality of requirements and specifications
- test coverage
- stability of the system
- outstanding incidents

7. Select the UAT team (see Chapter 4)

- decide key roles

- business analyst
- testing specialist (with experience)
- tool specialist
- decide budget for staff
- decide skill requirements
- decide to hire or train skills
- create hiring specifications
- interview shortlist
- hire team
- identify training needs for each individual

8. Initiate UAT training (see Appendix C)

- decide training objectives
- in-house or external
- design or select course(s)
- provide introduction to UAT as a starter
- decide incremental training required
- draw up training programme

9. Form an initial project plan for UAT (see Chapter 6)

- identify key dates
- availability of RS
- availability of software/system to test
- availability of tools/environments
- UAT testing schedule
- planned release date

PLANNING THE UAT PROJECT CHECKLIST (UAT TEAM LEADER)

1. Identify the method of software/system acquisition to determine the best approach to UAT (see Chapter 1):

- in-house
- outsource
- COTS
- license

2. Ascertain whether the business intent and the user expectations have been captured and are measurable (see Chapters 2 and 6)

3. Verify that business requirements have been captured (see Chapters 2 and 6)

- unambiguous
- correct
- implementable
- necessary
- verifiable
- prioritised

4. Verify that all the requirements types are included (see Chapter 2)

- functional
- informational
- behavioural
- environmental

5. Write the acceptance criteria or check that the acceptance criteria are appropriate (see Chapters 2 and 6)

6. Ensure the scope is relevant, clear and unambiguous (see Chapter 2)

7. Capture or verify the business processes (see Chapters 2 and 6)

8. Evaluate the current documentation and its suitability to serve as a test basis (see Chapter 6)

9. Establish the FTP and TDP as the processes to be followed for UAT testing and the creation of the test documentation (see Chapter 3)

10. Build a plan to establish an adequate test basis and test using the FTP and TDP approach. Allow for regression testing and defect investigation/rework/retest (see Chapter 6)

11. Identify effort and elapsed time for UAT and any impact on the currently scheduled delivery date and report to the sponsor (see Chapter 6)

12. Ensure management controls are in place for test documentation and in preparation for test execution (see Chapter 6)

- version control
- IM
- test logging

UAT TEST DESIGN CHECKLIST

1. Establish the entry criteria for UAT (see Chapter 6)

2. Review test scripts where available (see Chapters 3 and 6)

3. Define the UAT strategy (see Chapters 3 and 7)

4. Review existing test conditions where available and write new test conditions (see Chapters 3 and 7)

   - uniquely referenced to requirements
   - at least one per requirement
   - logical statements that can be verified by testing
   - only outcomes are true or false
   - all test conditions for a requirement must be true

5. Review existing test cases where available and create new test cases based on the test conditions (see Chapters 3 and 7)
   - uniquely referenced to test conditions
   - test design techniques
     - EP
     - BVA
     - use case testing
   - test by process
   - test by data sequence
   - test by post-condition and precondition match
   - test by time sequence
   - test by priority

6. Write test scripts based on the test cases (see Chapters 3 and 7)

   - uniquely referenced to test cases
   - high level test scripts or detailed test scripts
     - depends on the test
     - depends on the tester
   - test data included or referenced

7. Test coverage requirements (see Chapters 3 and 7)

- minimum would be requirements coverage
- coverage can be by functions or structure
- essential to ensure adequate testing is achieved
- only effective measure of how much testing has been done

UAT TEST EXECUTION CHECKLIST

1. Check availability of test environment(s) (see Chapters 1, 6 and 8)

2. Define high level test schedule against UAT strategy to achieve priorities, e.g. risk based (see Chapter 8)

3. Define detailed test schedule to achieve best use of resources (people, environments, skills) and best completion date (see Chapter 8)

4. Ensure the test log is kept up to date (see Chapter 8)

- captures all tests to be run
- records results and any retesting to be done
- adds regression testing as necessary
- revised to accommodate all retesting requirements

5. Ensure incidents are being reported accurately and in good time (see Chapter 8)

- IM process
- incidents logged and reported to development
- confirmed defects retested after correction
- regression requirements decided after correction
- test schedule log updated

6. Check regularly on defect resolution with development team and ensure there are no bottlenecks

7. Generate regular test summary reports to identify

    a. progress against plan
    b. coverage achieved to date
    c. incidents reported and resolved
    d. outstanding incidents
    e. progress against acceptance criteria
    f. estimated completion based on performance to date (see Chapter 8)

UAT RELEASE DECISION CHECKLIST

1. Identify status against acceptance criteria (see Chapter 9).

- test coverage
- requirements coverage
- defects outstanding

2. Identify effort/time required to meet acceptance criteria in full

3. Examine alternatives based on residual risk (see Chapter 9)

- delay system release (if timing is not critical)
- define workarounds (avoid problems by changing process)
- revise acceptance criteria (if reduced quality is an option)
- review contingency plans for release (plan to minimize impact of problems, e.g. additional help and technical support services)

4. Emergency -release criteria to enable controlled release (see Chapter 9)

- stability
- usability
- coverage

5. Report status to key stakeholders with alternative proposals for release (see Chapter 9).

6. Prepare UAT completion report with recommendations (see Chapter 9)

POST-UAT ACTIONS CHECKLIST

1. User training design and plan (see Chapter 10)

- built on UAT training
- learn from UAT
- train workarounds
- include information for anticipated FAQs

2. Post-release support (see Chapter 10)

- help desk
- technical support
- FAQs

3. Continue testing (see Chapter 10)

- complete outstanding tests after initial release to reduce risk
- incorporate reliability growth if necessary
- monitor defects corrected and new incidents reported

4. Post-UAT report with details for FAQs etc. (see Chapter 10)

- capture all the actions and decisions
- report designed as an input to 'lessons learned'

APPENDIX B
ANSWERS AND COMMENTS

CHAPTER 1

Answers to what have you learned

Q1 B

Answer A is incorrect. UAT may take longer but usually takes less time than other testing.

Answer C is incorrect. UAT evaluates the system against business requirements (not necessarily captured in the requirements specification), business processes and user expectations.

Answer D is incorrect. UAT is formal testing.

Q2 B, D, E

Answer A is incorrect. Technical specifications are used for testing during development, but not for UAT because they have a technical perspective rather than a user perspective.

Answer C is incorrect. Business requirements are part of the basis for UAT but they may not be defined fully in a requirements specification.

Answer F is incorrect. There would be no value in repeating tests already run for system testing.

Answer G is incorrect. While tests could be automated they should not be designed by developers because UAT must be from an end-user perspective.

Q3 C, D, F

Answer A is incorrect. It may or may not be a true statement but it is not the reason users carry out UAT.

Answer B is incorrect. Users may or may not be experts on technical performance but it is not the reason they carry out UAT.

Answer E is incorrect. Developer testing is essential but it is different from UAT and both levels of testing are needed.

Our responses to questions to consider

1. What questions would you ask if your organisation asked you to carry out UAT on a new piece of software that is being introduced to support the sales activity in your business?

There are a number of key questions that the person conducting the UAT should ask, especially if there has been no previous involvement with the project. For example:

- What is the overall goal of the project?
- Who are the stakeholders?
- What stage of development is the project in?
- When will UAT (provisionally) take place?
- Is the project based on a waterfall or agile model?
- Is there a contract related to the acceptance of the criteria?
- Have the stakeholders been involved and have they bought into the project?
- Do the requirements reflect the current business need?

The aim must be to have a system that makes sales people more effective, so you will need sales people to be involved. They will probably be busy selling and will not want to run tests, but you will need to at least engage them in a conversation about what they need and expect.

2. How would you react if your boss told you that the development project for which you will be doing UAT is running late and he wants you to do UAT in parallel with the developers completing the development?

Running UAT in parallel with development is not only a waste of time and effort (because the system is likely to be changing from day to day), but also can provide a false sense of security. Even if the UA tests were passed successfully, that would be no guarantee that what was actually delivered at the end would work. On the other hand, there may be some value in having users familiarise themselves with the system during development – as long as this does not get in the way of development!

It is important for the success of the project as a whole that the value and purpose of UAT is understood as well as the entry and exit criteria. If the manager is not aware of the reasons for these restrictions, it is important to point them out. They may not realise that running in parallel with development will compromise the value of UAT and overall may be the source of greater delays.

3. Why not just get professional testers to do UAT? After all they have experience of formal testing and know all the techniques.

Successful UAT is the result of bringing together expertise about the business and its existing processes, expertise about the new system and how it will work, and UAT expertise. As the name suggests, the purpose of the testing is that the user accepts the system and this is not normally possible without the user taking part. Testing specialists carrying out testing will also introduce a bias in that they are likely to test how they know the system works as opposed to how the users will use it, simply because they lack the experience and the knowledge to recreate what a user would do. In some cases, where users cannot carry out UAT, it may be possible for users to specify exactly what ought to be tested to achieve acceptance and have others carry out the testing, although this will always represent a compromise to the quality of the UAT.

CHAPTER 2

Exercise 2.1

1. The requirement relates to all requests staff make for expenses, purchase orders, absence and so on.
2. The requirement does not relate to changes made by staff that do not require approval such as updating address or bank account details.
3. The requirement states that once the request has been made (saved) the requester should receive notification of any updates in status or other changes to the request.
4. The requirement is ranked in terms of importance but we cannot tell from a single requirement whether this is a ranking that relates to the whole RS, and is therefore the 34th most important requirement in the RS, or whether it is a ranking that relates to the section within the requirements it belongs to.
5. The requirement is of high priority.

Answers to what have you learned

Q1 A

Answer B is incorrect. Business intent is independent of UAT and would be needed even if UAT were not happening.

Answer C is incorrect, although it is another important aspect of the system that is tested at UAT.

Answer D is incorrect. The purpose of the business is the overall reason for the business to exist. Business intent is the reason for building or changing an IS within that business.

Q2 C

Answer A is incorrect. Business requirements are a significant part of the test basis for UAT but the strategy defines how we will test for acceptance.

Answer B is incorrect. Although business requirements form part of the UA test basis they are not the complete test basis (user expectations form another part of the UA test basis).

Answer D is incorrect because answer B is incorrect.

Q3 D

Answers A, B and C are all possible limitations of requirements, so answer D is the best answer.

Q4 B

Answer A is incorrect. Requirements need to have enough relevant detail to make them clear, although unnecessary detail must be avoided because it will make the requirement unclear.

Answer C is incorrect. The level of technical detail will vary between requirements but requirements are about user needs so should be expressed in user terms. This does not necessarily make them non-technical (for example the user may be an engineer and need technical details in the requirements) but technical detail should be kept to the minimum consistent with clarity and readability.

Answer D is incorrect. It is a description of a good requirement.

Our responses to questions to consider

1. You are a stakeholder new to the project and are asked to read the RS to get an idea of what the project is about, but you do not understand some, most or all of the requirements. What would you do?

It would be a good idea to check first with your teammates and team leader to see what level of understanding you are expected to need. If there has been specific training set up for UAT, you would clearly benefit from it; if not, you might like to suggest that something is put in place. If all else fails you can consult the users, developers and business analysts as appropriate, but remember they are likely to be busy people.

You will need a good understanding of the requirements to be able to design and/or implement tests. If you think this might be an issue you need to flag it.

2. What is the difference between an RS and a UA test basis?

An RS is the formal expression of requirements that has been documented for development and that may have been subsequently updated. A test basis for UAT is the set of documents needed to enable UA tests to be designed and implemented. The test basis will need to include a definition of user expectations and a description of business processes as well as an up-to-date version of the business requirements with any changes made since the document was initially approved. So a UA test basis typically updates and extends the RS.

CHAPTER 3

Answers to what have you learned

Q1 A *(strictly A is functional coverage but it is the only answer that relates to the test coverage idea)*

Answer B is incorrect. It simply counts total tests run and has no direct connection with coverage.

Answer C is incorrect. Tests are normally designed to achieve a single test objective.

Answer D is incorrect. Scope is the breadth of testing, which is a different kind of measure of what is and is not tested. Test coverage measures how much of the in-scope functionality has been covered by testing.

Q2 D

Answer A may be true but is not the correct answer because it is not a benefit of reviews as a means of evaluating documents.

Answer B is incorrect. Reviews are not inexpensive; in fact they soak up valuable effort, which is why they must be effective in finding defects.

Answer C is incorrect. Reviews can only expect to find some of the defects but enough to make the effort worthwhile because the cost of finding the defects any other way or of not finding the defects would be higher.

Q3 B

Answer A is incorrect. Test techniques exploit what happens when users enter non-valid data to identify defects but do not affect what users can enter.

Answer C is incorrect. Boundaries are the edges of partitions rather than extreme conditions. Some boundaries may be at extremes, for instance the highest value a system can handle, but the test is a boundary test because it is at the edge of a partition rather than because it is using extreme values.

Answer D is incorrect. Only those test cases that are outside a boundary should fail, while those inside or on the boundary should pass.

Our responses to questions to consider

1. Your organisation is reluctant to allow UA testers to be part of a review process. What would be the best way to overcome that reluctance?

It would be useful to find out the cause of this reluctance. Is the worry caused by a fear of overcrowding or a fear of certain objections being raised that may delay the project? The original CHAOS report showed that the second most common cause for project failure was lack of involvement. The review process aims to make sure that the requirements match the needs of the business and the business ought to be involved in this process.

Even if the other stakeholders are part of the review, users or a user representative in the form of a subject-matter expert being present will help to achieve the aim of the review. It may be useful for everyone involved in the review to understand its aims and to have the message reinforced that no decisions need to be made in the review as to what changes are required to the system, only to establish what the current need is.

2. You are being offered a training course before starting work as a UA tester. What would be your requirements for a one-day course? Suppose you could have three days of training. What changes would you make to your requirements?

This is a tough call but worth thinking about. We'll be offering some help in Chapters 4 and 5 but now would be a good time to think about what you would need to cope with UAT in your own organisation. If you have a look at the content of publicly available courses, for example, you can get an idea of what is typically delivered and identify what would be gaps for you. Areas such as getting to know the system you will be testing, understanding how your development team has tested the system and becoming familiar with any tools you may be expected to use are all areas that generic courses cannot provide. You will need to find a way to get this information for yourself.

Timing is everything. One day is not very much time to fit in all that you might want to learn about to feel ready to test, but it is still a good idea to distil your ideas down and see what could be fitted into one day. Then give yourself the luxury of three days and consider how you might do it differently. These thought experiments will set you up well for the material in Chapters 4 and 5 on building and training an effective UAT team.

You already have the most important knowledge because you are a user. Probably the best value for your one day would come from gaining familiarity with requirements (take some of your own to make sure you get some practical value from the training). The second thing would be to learn how to get the best from reviews. You can pick up some basic testing knowledge from books.

In a three-day course you could add some testing basics, but the main benefit of the extra time would be to enable you to get some practice in reviewing and in writing test scripts (if possible, based on your own requirements).

CHAPTER 4

Answers to what have you learned

Q1 A

Answers B, C and D are all incorrect because these are roles that are external to UAT, although they need to have a very close relationship. They all have wider responsibilities but we would expect them to provide help and support as needed.

Q2 A

The correct sequence is forming, storming, norming, performing.

Q3 B, D

Answer A is incorrect although still very important. Written job descriptions should provide everyone with a clear sense of what is expected from them, which is important to team effectiveness.

Answer C is incorrect. It may be appropriate for those with technical skills to take the lead on occasions but that is usually in the interests of progressing the task rather than building team spirit.

Answer E is incorrect. It is an important rule for leaders to be clear and decisive, and a good leader has the best chance of building an effective team, but leadership skills are part of separating the leader from the team rather than building team spirit.

Our responses to questions to consider

1. Your most knowledgeable UA tester has been identified as a complainer. What would you do?

There is a choice here between trying to 'keep the peace' and taking an opportunity to build the team's morale. If you ignore the complaints, you could demotivate a good tester. If you respond to the complaints (perhaps at the expense of time to do other important things), you give the complainer a sense of increased importance and perhaps create tensions within the team. Keeping the peace options are fraught with danger.

If you spend some time with the complainer, one to one, and try to understand the underlying problems that lead to complaints, you may discover genuine issues that need to be resolved. One way to move the situation forward might be to give the complainer the opportunity to be the team's spokesperson in resolving the issues on behalf of the team – and of course tell the team to take their issues to the new spokesperson.

2. One team member is being regularly distracted by their line manager to do routine tasks. How would you deal with this situation?

This is a common challenge. It points to one of two possible scenarios: either the team member is genuinely too busy in their 'day job' to be able to commit enough time to UAT or the line manager is unwilling to manage without a staff member and is asserting their authority to make life difficult for the team. Either way a frank discussion with the line manager should uncover the truth and provide a way forward. If the problem really is overload, a replacement should be sought and the original team member released. If the problem is one of attitude, it needs to be challenged and, if necessary, escalated.

3. Your company does not have space to house the UAT team away from the rest of the business but is willing to give the team half of each day to work on UAT. How would you organise the team to work?

This is far from ideal but it does at least provide an opportunity for some daily team time. If a suitable location can be found, there is an opportunity to create some 'team space'. Somewhere like a local community hall or even a back room in a pub (that is not open all day) can be a good meeting place. There will be a small hire cost but for that you may have the chance to store things at the venue so you can make the place feel like the team's home.

4. Your company provides a room for the UAT team to work in but takes the view that all your normal work must be completed as usual during UAT. How would you ensure that the UAT meets its deadlines?

Clearly the team needs a routine so that everyone is available at the same time when necessary, although there may equally be times when we want to stagger the working hours. During planning, for example, we will want the whole team together. During test execution it may be more attractive to have an extended working day with the team split in half, with a handover in the middle of the extended day. This will require good team discipline so that time is not wasted, and good cooperation with the business to ensure normal work is not being neglected, so regular communication between the team leader and the rest of the business is important.

CHAPTER 5

Our responses to questions to consider

The project you are working on is acquiring a COTS-based suite of applications configured to meet your company's needs, but there are some known potential gaps in functionality. Implementation is scheduled for 12 months ahead and a UAT team will be formed 1 month before UAT.

a. As UAT team leader elect you have been asked to review the plans. What feedback would you give?

There are a few challenges here. The COTS approach means a contractual acceptance as well as an internal one, and payment will have to be made on contractual acceptance so it needs to be thorough. The team will need to get up to speed with the COTS modules and also have a strong grasp of the requirements before UAT, which points to early training and a start on the requirements review and learning at least three months before UAT. It is all a question of risk. Is it worth forming a team earlier to get a good start or take the risk of accepting a system by default because testing is not good enough to demonstrate weaknesses?

b. As a nominated end-user tester for the UAT team, what would you propose?

As an end-user I know I'm going to be asked to continue with my 'day job' while I prepare for UAT. In that case the earlier I can start on the preparation work the better so I can stagger it over a longer period. I will need some training just before I start the requirements review so I would propose that training is arranged for the team as soon as requirements are available for review, then the team is given an allowance of time over a period to get the review done and begin preparing the tests.

CHAPTER 6

Exercise 6.1

A4.0 – Ambiguous, 'colleagues' should be replaced with some reference to the user hierarchy, for instance members of the team as defined in the user hierarchy. Contains two requirements: that the calendar is visible to the user, containing the right information, and that it must be visible at a particular point in the absence process. Too focused on how the solution ought to work.

A4.1 – Can be broken down into two requirements: that the system should show the existing balance of remaining days off and that the system should recalculate the new balance after placing the planned days off in the calendar.

A4.2 – OK.

A4.3 – OK.

A4.4 – Ambiguous, should refer to what the holiday year is, for example January to December or a year from the start date of the user.

A4.5 – Poorly defined, reference to other requirement without referring to the unique ID.

A4.6 – Contains two requirements.

A4.7 – Poorly defined, should refer to the user hierarchy and contains multiple requirements.

A4.8 – Ambiguous, should not contain the word 'soon', but rather define a specific time period. Focused on the solution as opposed to the need in referring to a 'system reminder'.

Exercise 6.2

There are at least three other potential user stories that could have been used in the case study example but were not for the sake of brevity. User story 1.1 is fairly straightforward and represents existing functionality within the system. UAT will now include the tests that ensure someone logged on with a manager role will be able to send expenses for approval. There may be other managerial roles that need to be tested that were not included. User stories 2.1, 2.2 and 2.3 relate to assigning an account so that one user can manage tasks on another user's behalf. User story 2.3 hinted at the fact that the manager and assistant relationship may not be the only one that could benefit from the ability to assign accounts. Other user stories could be created around assigning accounts to deal with absence for a number of different roles in the organisation. User stories 3.1 and 3.2 deal with third-party billing and how this is recorded on the accounts system. In the case of third-party billing, additional contract details may be required, for instance the third-party address. If this is the case, the system will have to deal with what happens to the third-party billing address if the contract is subsequently changed as is described in use case 3.2. There may also be other roles that need to be able to select or deselect the third-party billing option and may have to be able to edit the contract in other ways, specifically related to the tax for the purposes of the accounts payable department.

Answers to what have you learned

Q1 C

Answer A is incorrect. This is an impossible objective and needs to be qualified (for example no critical defects).

Answer B is incorrect. This is also an impossible objective to achieve because not all risks will be known and it will not be possible to eliminate all known risks. A more reasonable target would be to reduce the known risks to an acceptable level.

Answer D is incorrect. It may not be possible to complete everything in the UAT plan as originally agreed. Some aspects will be essential (for example achieving acceptable test coverage) and these need to be specifically stated.

Q2 D, E

Answer A is incorrect. It may not be possible to complete all planned testing but the testing completed may provide adequate test coverage.

Answer B is incorrect. Change requests can come in at any time and will continue to arrive after release of the system. They have no bearing on release unless a change is deemed essential, and that would only arise in UAT if it was related to a critical defect of some kind.

Answer C is incorrect but tempting. Normally all test incidents would be at least investigated before release, even if not cleared. Technically a test incident is outstanding until it is cleared, but if investigation showed, for example, that the failed test was due to an error in the test script there would be no reason to delay release.

Q3 A, D, E

Answers B and C are incorrect because they are techniques for expressing requirements and not requirements in themselves. Typically user stories might be used to capture undocumented user expectations and use cases might be used to capture undocumented business processes.

Answer F is incorrect. Technical specifications would be part of the test basis for system testing but not for UAT.

Our responses to questions to consider

1. You are finding that users are reluctant to express ideas about what they expect from the system when it is delivered and fall back on what is in the requirements. What would you do?

The reaction is common where users are either not fully engaged with the changes that the new system will bring or are not well informed about what will happen. They may be expressing lack of interest or lack of knowledge. Either way it would be useful to try to find out why because the outcome could be a system that they are unhappy with or cannot use.

2. The sales manager believes that acceptance criteria should not delay delivery to customers who have expectations of early delivery. The development manager believes that acceptance criteria should include only requirements coverage. The marketing manager is concerned about the image of the business and insists on zero serious defects as an acceptance criterion. What should you do?

Conflicting priorities are not unusual but they need to be harmonised or you will have no secure basis for acceptance. A workshop involving all the stakeholders can be a very good vehicle for flushing out such disagreements and getting a resolution.

All three of the roles are seeking to minimise the impact on their own area of responsibility and do what they believe is best for the business. There is always a compromise position, especially if the individuals are willing to work together to resolve any problems and minimise impact for each other.

3. The development team is reluctant to give the UAT team access to the incident reporting system because it could result in lost incident data if someone makes a mistake. What would you do?

An understandable concern. Until the system is released into UAT the development team has ownership and control, but this might be a good time to ask the development team to provide some training on the tools so that end-users are less likely to make mistakes when they use them. The training may build confidence enough to encourage the development team to allow access before UAT begins, or you may discover that additional controls are needed to prevent any data loss.

CHAPTER 7

Question 7.1

There is no link between the two test scripts that makes it logical to carry out the first test and then the second using the same UA tester. The output from one script is not equal to or part of the input for the second script. In essence both are checking the same screen for the correct information but logged in as different roles. If there is time to do so, UAT should test the whole contract process end to end. It may therefore be useful to have one tester logged on as the team member and one as the team manager (ideally testers who are a team member and team manager) where they use the same contract, created by the team member, and follow it through all the stages of the process together. The team member can send the contract for approval and the manager can approve it, while they both check that the screens used are correct according to the requirements. A number of alternative processes may be tested including rejection of the contract, which represents an alternative path. If the test scripts were carried out in sequence by the same tester, the tester would have to log off as the team member and log on again as the team manager, which would be time-consuming and also does not, in our example, represent how users will use the system in real life.

Question 7.2

There are an almost infinite number of entries that do not meet the criteria of the example of the allowed entry and therefore represents a negative test. The number can be limited to certain types of negative tests and refined by using user- or tester-generated scenarios that represent the kinds of mistakes users are most likely to make:

1. Wrong number of characters; according to BVA we may try 0, 1, 6 and 7 characters.
2. Leaving a required field empty; already covered by the zero characters entry in the previous example.
3. The wrong type of character, * & = -; we want to try to find the most likely candidates, for instance a foreign alphabetical character such as é.
4. A capital letter.
5. Any character produced by inserting a valid character but with the shift or control key depressed at the same time.

Answers to what have you learned

Q1 A

Answer B is incorrect. Traceability is a mechanism and not a measure.

Answer C is incorrect. Traceability could ensure that there is a test of each requirement but not that the test data are complete.

Answer D is incorrect. It is important for traceability that each requirement has a unique ID but traceability is not the means of achieving it.

Q2 C

Answer A is incorrect. This is a test precondition.

Answer B is incorrect. Collections of features are not called test conditions.

Answer D is incorrect. Exit criteria are not the same as test conditions.

Q3 A, C, D

Answer B is incorrect. Tester availability is not related to test design but is a planning factor.

Answer E is incorrect. Risk is a key driver of test strategy and may be used to prioritise tests but individual UA test cases are mostly directed at requirements, processes and user interfaces.

Q4 C

Answer A is incorrect. BVA does help to minimise the total test cases but not all of these are negative.

Answer B is incorrect. BVA does not identify all negative test cases. In fact no technique can do that; the number is potentially very large.

Answer D is incorrect. Boundaries identify the edges of partitions but BVA is applied to test at the boundaries, not to identify them.

Our response to questions to consider

1. The test cases have been created. When deciding what order they should be placed in, the project manager wants you to focus on risk and the project sponsor wants you to focus on processes. How do you decide what order they should be placed in?

It is most important to know what the project manager means by risk and therefore what risks they want to mitigate. There may be a part of the system that is key to success or failure, will have the biggest financial impact if it fails or that may be a part of the system that is seen as high profile. The business processes may already cover the high-risk and high-profile functionality. If they do not, ensure that the project manager and the other stakeholders come to a consensus on the issue of what ought to be tested first. If the parts of the system that are considered the highest risk are part of the day-to-day processes, the two approaches can be combined, along with any other considerations you would like to include, to create an approach that meets the criteria of the project manager and the sponsor.

2. On the first day of UAT half the team are off ill with a cold. What decision would you make about whether to run testing? What tests do you think you could run?

You may need to do a little investigation and separate the processes that require input from the whole group or that are complex and need a number of different users to test together from those that are simple or that stand alone. If this work will take a lot of time or would be very disruptive to testing, UAT may need to be postponed.

CHAPTER 8

Exercise 8.1

1. In our example, in test script #1 the tester is logged on with a user role that is not allowed to access the Contracts module and in test script #2 the tester is logged on with a user role that is allowed access to the Contracts module. It would not be efficient to have these test scripts follow one another in the same scenario because it would involve logging off and logging back on again. It would be more useful to add each script to a set of tests that require this log on.

2. If possible, the tests should be included in the process or processes that cover the contracts functionality. As different roles are required to test this process and those roles have a part to play in progressing it, the check for the logon to the module could sit at the start of the contracts process tests for those different roles. Because they need to log on to access the module in order to use it, they can test this functionality at the same time.

Answers to what have you learned

Q1 D

Answers A, B and C are not incorrect but only answer D is complete.

Q2 D

Answer A is correct but incomplete.

Answer B is incorrect. Since the test script has been created it is part of the formal test documentation and we will need a record of the test failure and subsequent correction.

Answer C is incorrect for the same reasons as B.

Q3 B

Answer A is incorrect. This is an estimate.

Answer C is incorrect. Incidents can be recorded on a test log but they are not the only information recorded.

Answer D is incorrect. As with C, this is correct but not complete.

Our response to question to consider

1. Halfway through testing you are asked to provide a fixed date for finishing UAT. What would your answer to this request be?

It is possible to provide an estimate of the time required to finish UAT based on the time it took to complete the first half of UAT. It does not provide a guarantee, because issues may arise that are unexpected and perhaps critical that did not occur in the first half of the testing. If a fixed date is required, it comes with the risk that not all of the testing will be completed. It is important to establish that this risk exists and that it represents a smaller or otherwise more acceptable risk than missing the deadline would have. If the acceptance criteria include a coverage percentage that is required for UAT sign-off and the omitted testing affects the coverage percentage that can be achieved, the acceptance criteria also need to be adjusted.

We should have learned from the first half of UAT. If any delays were due to incidents and defect corrections, we could estimate the likely impact of a similar level of incidents in the second half of UAT (or scale the impact according to whether we think the second half is likely to have more or less challenges). If delays were caused by shortages of staff, equipment or skills, we can identify whether these problems have been resolved and estimate accordingly.

CHAPTER 9

Answers to what have you learned

Q1 D, E, F

Answer A is incorrect. This is part of the decision logic but not one that determines acceptance.

Answer B is incorrect. This may well be a challenge but it does not automatically determine acceptance.

Answer C is incorrect. This is also part of the decision logic but does not determine acceptance.

Q2 D

Answer A is incorrect. A risk-based testing strategy helps to mitigate risk but if testing is finished early, the strategy may not have been completely implemented.

Answer B is incorrect. Continuous evaluation is important to identify progress towards acceptance criteria but this does not mitigate risk if testing is finished early.

Answer C is incorrect. All activities in UAT contribute to the eventual risk outcome. Identifying a risk-based test strategy, for example, is a key step.

Answer D is the best answer because it combines a risk-based approach with continuous evaluation so that risk mitigation can be monitored and an informed judgement made if testing has to stop.

Q3 D

Answers A, B and C are all more or less likely. If UAT has progressed to a risk assessment then it is very unlikely to be seriously flawed; the cost of continuing development and testing to this stage would be very high for a system with major problems and action would have been taken earlier, so outright rejection is unlikely.

Our response to questions to consider

1. The test manager wants to set up a meeting to discuss the release towards the end of UAT. Who should they invite and why?

There are two sets of interested parties, those involved in UAT and the stakeholders. Representatives from both groups should be present. The meeting should ideally not be the first communication on the success and the progress of testing. Those involved in UAT should be prepared to interpret the UAT results in a way that is meaningful to making a release decision, and the stakeholders should be prepared to make a decision based on the data. The more relevant points of view that are present, the more likely the meeting is to reach a suitable conclusion.

2. There are a number of critical defects still outstanding. What does this mean in terms of the risk of release and to the release decision?

It would be hard to come to any conclusions about the release of a system while critical faults are unresolved. The only release decision that should be made is to either not release or to defer releasing the system while the critical errors are fixed. It is also hard to assess the progress of UAT in these circumstances as critical errors usually stop other testing from taking place and regression testing is also likely to be required. The risk of release at this stage is high and the system will not work as it was intended or in any other meaningful way.

The questions and comments represent a useful resource for the creation of FAQ content and will provide valuable information to support business as usual (BAU) staff as well as the end-user trainer.

APPENDIX C
UAT TRAINING

THE TRAINING PROCESS

Training is, first and foremost in the implementation of an IS project, a process of enabling. One-off classroom courses have a place in this process but so do a variety of other methods that are less about 'pushing' information and more about helping individuals and teams to acquire the knowledge and skills they need to be effective.

The generic process is one of:

- defining training objectives;
- identifying the best way to achieve the objectives;
- delivering the training;
- measuring the learning achieved.

This process can be broken down into as many elements of training as necessary and, helped by the feedback from measurement, can be repeated as often as required. This is very important. Where changes of perception or acquisition of new skills are concerned, a single training event will never fully meet the need. Timing is key, and training can often be broken into three key stages:

- preparation – concentrating on information and motivation for the next stage;
- delivery – concentrating on providing skills and knowledge required;
- reinforcement – concentrating on refreshing skills and knowledge and, if appropriate, advancing the level.

Each of these stages can involve the receivers of training directly in identifying needs, especially between stages, so that training delivery can be tailored to the individuals and their needs at each delivery.

Because training events are not all about 'push', the best method of delivery will, in many cases, not be teaching or lecturing, and much of the training delivery will be achieved more effectively by participants in the project rather than training specialists. Where a training specialist is essential is in helping to shape and define the overall training programme; a role we will call training consultant.

THE TRAINING CONSULTANT ROLE

The training process must be integrated into the overall project plan and can be understood as a series of tasks, some required and others optional, that should be carried out depending on the size and specific circumstances of the project.

Figure C.1 lists the high-level tasks that need to be carried out in order to deliver UAT and end-user training. Tasks in italics are not directly training related but are research tasks that help the training consultant to understand the system. Research tasks may include reading the relevant documentation, helping with the UAT preparation and attending demonstrations and walk-throughs.

The training consultant is not necessarily a specialist trainer and not necessarily a consultant in the usual sense of the word. The role is one of enabling, shaping, encouraging, motivating, measuring progress, adapting and partly delivering a training programme. The consultant must therefore be someone who knows the organisation and the project well, understands the challenges of IS implementation, has experience of training delivery, and can manage a programme over an extended period. This is, therefore, a senior role in the project with a very high level of responsibility and accountability for the eventual success of the project.

Even if an IS implementation is small, the training consultant role is vital although it may be absorbed within another role, such as the project manager role, or provided by an external specialist on a part-time basis.

This is not a book about training so we will not pursue the development of a project-wide training programme here, but UAT training is a key part of preparation for UAT so we will focus attention on defining that part of the training programme to provide a flavour of the remainder of the overall programme.

It is also very useful to understand how UAT training should be planned, prepared, delivered and followed up in the context of the overall training process for a number of reasons:

- The person who delivers or enables UAT training will also be likely to deliver or enable other training for the project.
- The end-user training, which is as critical to the success of implementation as UAT training, will be partially dependent on UAT training and testing (and its outcomes) as a baseline for the end-user training content.
- Planning for the training activities is likely to be done at the same time.

UAT training has four key objectives:

1. to provide a thorough understanding of the UAT process to be used on the project and its relationship with the development process;
2. to provide a thorough grasp of the system under test and the business intent for which it is being implemented; this will include familiarity with the relevant documentation, especially the RS;

Figure C.1 The training process

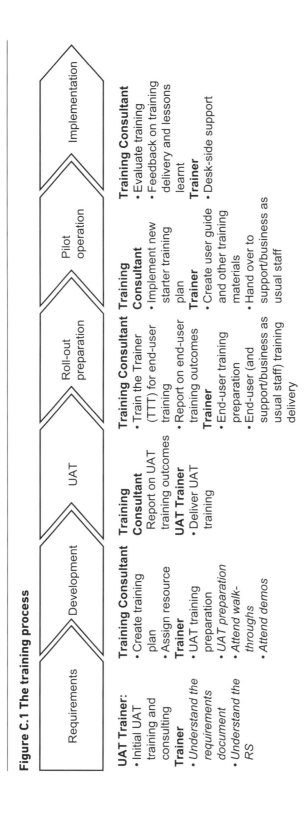

Requirements	Development	UAT	Roll-out preparation	Pilot operation	Implementation

UAT Trainer:
- Initial UAT training and consulting

Trainer
- *Understand the requirements document*
- *Understand the RS*

Training Consultant
- Create training plan
- Assign resource

Trainer
- UAT training preparation
- *UAT preparation*
- *Attend walk-throughs*
- *Attend demos*

Training Consultant
- Report on UAT training outcomes

UAT Trainer
- Deliver UAT training

Training Consultant
- Train the Trainer (TTT) for end-user training
- Report on end-user training outcomes

Trainer
- End-user training preparation
- End-user (and support/business as usual staff) training delivery

Training Consultant
- Implement new starter training plan

Trainer
- Create user guide and other training materials
- Hand over to support/business as usual staff

Training Consultant
- Evaluate training
- Feedback on training delivery and lessons learnt

Trainer
- Desk-side support

3. to prepare the participants fully for the tasks they are about to carry out including key skills such as review techniques, test design and execution, and reporting, and it must include an introduction to any management tools (for example IM) that they will have to use;

4. to promote UAT team formation and development.

Clearly timing is essential in planning and delivering these training events. Objective 1 must be delivered early in the project. Objectives 2 and 3 will need to be close to the beginning of the UAT exercise, partly because the system will need to be ready for demonstration and partly because the time lapse between training and use of the skills must be minimised. Objective 4 should, ideally, be a feature of all other training.

These objectives set a rough timetable that might look like this:

- An early training phase to achieve objective 1 and initiate team development (which requires the UAT team to be identified and staffed early in the project).

- A second training phase to introduce the system and testing some time before completion of development and further enhance team formation, after which the team can begin key tasks such as requirements reviews.

- A practical demonstration of the system and hands-on testing training just before UAT begins, together with hands-on training of any required management tools. (Team development can be further enhanced here through role play based on realistic scenarios.)

- Workshop sessions can be arranged during the UAT phase to sharpen skills or introduce specific techniques that can be used in this project.

- A UAT review session to elicit feedback on the effectiveness of UAT training and of UAT, and to identify key insights into what will be most important for end-user training. In particular, the UA testers may have discovered potentially serious issues for which workarounds have been developed during UAT.

The individual trainers for these sessions can be drawn from the project team, from specialist trainers inside or outside the organisation and from the sponsor and managers who defined the business benefits. The widest possible participation in training delivery should be encouraged, with the training consultant acting as the coordinator and ensuring that all training is effective and integrated into a clear programme.

By way of an example of more detailed planning we will examine the requirements for training objective 2 above, using the template of:

- entry criteria (what must be in place to enable the training);
- training inputs (what must be provided at the start of the training event);
- training content (what the training event must deliver to participants);
- training outputs (what must be created by the training event).

The template provides a coherent structure for this and any training event.

Entry criteria for UAT training

Entry criteria are the conditions that must be met to make the training event viable.

Business requirements are available

Understanding the requirements is key to UAT as well as to UAT training. One purpose of this event is to enable the preparation of a UA test basis. (The next training event will deliver key skills for designing tests from the test basis.)

Application code is nearing completion

Often UAT training is carried out before work on the IS has been fully completed. This is acceptable as long as the 'workarounds' are known and there are not so many that they affect the usefulness of UA testing and training. The relationship between the business intent, the business requirements and the system as developed should be clear.

System testing is under way and all previous testing levels have been signed off

Previous testing must have been completed and outstanding issues must be of low criticality or of a cosmetic nature and a known quantity.

Training inputs for UAT training

Training inputs are the prerequisites for effective training.

Suitable training venue

A training venue must be suitable for the purpose, for example demonstrating a system, and large enough for the anticipated participants. The arrangements for acquiring suitable training venues may need to be started very early to ensure their availability when required.

Attendance list

The attendance list should provide each attendee's current role and their role within the UAT team. If possible a brief outline of the attendee's previous experience will help the trainer(s) form a mental picture.

Defined objectives

Defining the objectives for UAT training is essential. They need to be sent to the attendees in their invitations and should be the framework for the training content. Referring to the objectives of training should also keep the training content relevant.

Evaluation of current knowledge

The content of training must be relevant to the audience's current levels of UAT and business knowledge and experience. A brief quiz (used as an initial icebreaker) can be used to determine where each participant is (or thinks they are) on a scale against each key topic.

Training materials

Visuals, handouts, exercises and any supporting material should be bound into a manual bearing a suitable logo. A specific team logo is helpful in reinforcing the team's identity.

Trainer notes

Key words, phrases and exercises help to provide seamless delivery and, more importantly, to ensure no important points are missed in delivery.

UAT training content

General

An introduction to UAT and software testing will have been provided in an earlier training event (to meet objective 1).

Basics to cover would include:

- general project information and timeline;
- the basic functionality of the system;
- any known issues and workarounds;
- what the system is designed to deliver;
- what the expected business benefits are;
- what testing has already taken place;
- introduction and explanation of the RS.

Reinforcement may be needed for key ideas delivered in the earlier training event, such as:

- What is UAT?
- What is the specific purpose of UAT?
- What tasks are carried out during UAT and in what order?

These topics can be added to the content at appropriate stages as revision or used as an initial quiz to measure levels of current knowledge.

The interaction required to create the session, especially if members of the project team and other stakeholders deliver some of the material about the project, is invaluable in helping to form the 'UAT community'.

An introduction to the system, with demonstrations as necessary, is important so that the team can feel comfortable with the way the system works and, if possible, have an opportunity to do some simple practical exercises to gain confidence. Actual behaviour can also be related to the business requirement from which it arose to provide insights into the interpretation of the RS.

Task-based training

Detailed task-based training belongs under objective 3 and will be the focus of a later training event. All UA testers will need to understand the key steps in executing a test script, evaluating and logging the results, and reporting test incidents, so these ideas can be introduced in this training event to be reinforced with practical hands-on training at the next, which will be based on the specific approach to be used in the project.

At this stage some background will be needed on the overall processes so that testers can understand where their specific contribution fits. They will also need to understand the basics of how test scripts arise so that they can contribute their experience and question any aspect that does not make sense to them as end-users.

Key content will need to include:

- the FTP;
- requirements, test conditions, test cases, test scripts;
- how to complete a test script;
- what UAT test scripts will look like;
- how much detail they will contain;
- how to note issues on test scripts;
- how results are recorded;
- what a test incident is;
- how test incidents are reported;
- severity ratings and how to apply them.

The task-based training will need some background, such as:

- what will happen to issues raised;
- how to feed back issues that are not part of the script, such as usability;
- the importance of working independently and not forming a consensus.

By covering the points mentioned, the UA testers will have a good understanding of why and how they are taking part in UAT and what the outcomes will achieve.

Team formation

The single most important aspect of team formation is to ensure that the whole team is present. Exercises should provide opportunities for team members to cooperate and provide mutual help and support. Group practical exercises are one way to engage team members, although it is important to watch out for the least experienced or confident being marginalised by more confident team members.

Careful debriefing of exercises provides opportunities to draw out key issues about participation and mutual support by inviting participants to make their own assessments of how successful the exercise was and how each participant contributed.

Training outputs

Training outputs are those things we expect to see at the end of training to demonstrate that training was successful and to provide opportunities to enhance what has been learned.

Attendance list

A record of actual attendance, with some notes on participation by each trainee, may be useful later, especially if anyone has been forced to miss any part of the training.

Comments and questions list

Questions raise during training can be noted and fed back to those stakeholders who were not present. In particular, those not answered at the time can be followed up.

Completed exercises

Completed exercises from training may be useful to participants as a reminder of the situations in which key skills were practised. A record of completed exercises may also be a useful insight into the level of skills acquired during training and any that might need to be reinforced.

Increased knowledge and changed behaviour

The most important training output is the fact that the attendees have learned what they needed to learn from the session. The quiz at the start of training can be repeated to see how much participants' confidence in their knowledge has increased. Participant feedback can be collected and evaluated. The trainer can also provide feedback on the progress made by participants and any problems encountered.

REFERENCES

Adzic, G. (2009) *Bridging the communication gap: specification by example and agile acceptance testing.* London: Neuri Limited.

Hambling, B. and Samaroo, A. (2009) *Software testing: an ISEB Intermediate Certificate.* Swindon: BCS, The Chartered Institute for IT.

Hambling, B., Morgan, P., Samaroo, A., Thompson, G. and Williams, P. (2010) *Software testing: an ISTQB-ISEB Foundation Guide (2/e)*. Swindon: BCS, The Chartered Institute for IT.

House of Commons Transport Committee (2008) *The Opening of Heathrow Terminal 5: Twelfth Report of Session 2007–08*. Report number HC 543. London: Stationery Office.

South West Thames Regional Health Authority Communications Directorate (1993) *Report of the Inquiry into The London Ambulance Service* (February).

Tuckman, B. (1965) Developmental sequence in small groups. *Psychological Bulletin,* 63. 384–9.

INDEX

usability
  definition, 43, 164
  determination, 164
  prioritisation, 43, 46
  usability testing, 43, 47, 132
use cases
  definition, 52
  edge cases, 113–114, 129–130
  examples, 53, 112–114, 115–119
  purpose, 52, 112

user acceptance testing *see* UAT
user expectations
  capturing, 38, 51–52
  stakeholder interviews, 110
  testing, 46
user interfaces, test cases for, 71, 131–132
user processes, capturing, 110
user stories
  capturing, 111
  examples, 51–52, 111–112, 194

  meaning, 51
  value, costs and, 105–106

walk-throughs
  conduct, 108
  process, 72
  see also reviews
white-box testing, 59–60
workarounds, 40, 175
working environment, 89–90, 192–193
working patterns, 90, 192–193